STORYTELLING

Manipulation of the Audience - How to Learn to Skyrocket Your Personal Brand and Online Business Using the Power of Social Media Marketing, Including Instagram, Facebook and YouTube

By

DANIEL ANDERSON

medical or professional advice. The content within this book has been derived from various sources. Please consult a licensed professional before attempting any techniques outlined in this book.

By reading this document, the reader agrees that under no circumstances is the author responsible for any losses, direct or indirect, which are incurred as a result of the use of information contained within this document, including, but not limited to, — errors, omissions, or inaccuracies.

TABLE OF CONTENT

INTRODUCTION

Everybody and everything has a story. Some of them we study in schools in history classes, some we read for pleasure in the form of a novel, and most of them nowadays we consume in the form of movies, painting, music, architecture, and others. Today, the power of storytelling enters the businesses and becomes an indispensable skill for success.

A story is a narrative account of an event or a sequence of events. It can be true or fictional. But a good story always has a core element of truth, even if it is fiction. The message the story tells must be true. It must be consistent and authentic. A story adds emotion, characters and sensory details to plain facts. That's why a story grabs us, pulls us along its plot and delivers its key message powerfully.

Storytelling is the art to tell stories to engage an audience. The storyteller conveys a message, information, and knowledge, in an entertaining way. Literary techniques and nonverbal language are his tools.

The storytelling comes to us from ancient times. The spoken storytelling was the only way to share the experience of the communities and to get to know the world around at times before the appearance of media. The power of storytelling has been recognized and used by governments. One of the examples is the power of the church in medieval Europe, where the narration of the Bible held the population in fear and obedience. Moreover, the priests have been well known for their rhetoric skills. Even nowadays, in some countries, the content of history books is changed with the new governments getting to power. But the power of storytelling does not necessarily have to be abused. In most cases, the storytelling is used to promote science, and the method is being utilized by marketing as a new wave of product promotion.

In this book, you are going to see the power of stories and storytelling and also learn how to use in the different circumstances in your life.

HAPPY READING!!

CHAPTER 1: STORYTELLING AND ITS IMPORTANCE

Storytelling - A Time-Honored Tradition

Everyone likes a good story. From the olden days when the elderly would gather children and tell of stories of the past, to the modern groups at libraries where authors of books read their stories, storytelling is a time-honored tradition. What makes storytelling so exciting depends on the storyteller. If the storyteller is exciting and entertaining, then you can enjoy every minute of the story. The interesting part of storytelling is that most of the stories told are based on true events. This not only gives you an interesting story; it helps you learn something.

This honored tradition offers many adventures for all to enjoy. Everyone has a grandfather or grandmother who has told you that story of how they were in World War II or that they were part of the Women's right to vote. These stories not only offer knowledge and learning; they are part of your history. Learning about your ancestors through your immediate family is part of genealogy. Storytelling offers this much and more. Everyone likes to sit around and listen to their relative tell them about these types of stories. It gives them a sense of purpose because more often than not, stories always have a moral to whatever was being told.

Through storytelling there comes a chance of bonding. Bonding with family or friends is an important part of our lives. These are our partners in life, and it is always a good idea to draw knowledge from their experiences. There are times which storytelling is imagined and considered fiction, but because of the storyteller, the story gives entertainment. Having a good storyteller is vital for good storytelling. Many people in today's society forget this time-honored tradition.

Forgetting about storytelling is never a good idea. Without this tradition, there would be more television watching, video game playing, and all together waste of time. It is best to tell as many stories as you can to your children and grandchildren. Remembering this time-honored tradition will improve your attitude to stories.

Stories, Storytelling and the Healing Process

Lewis Carroll, the author of Alice in Wonderland, once called stories "love gifts." The power of stories combined by love provides the foundation for healing on many different levels. There are many in today's societies (worldwide) who have suffered many traumas and therefore need to hear the stories told with loving care. The storyteller, with every telling of healing stories, gives a precious gift. The stories told by the storyteller provide a means for people to strengthen themselves and begin to heal.

Sadly, there are many today that would dismiss storytelling as mere entertainment. The argument that the stories cannot possibly be true and that they are a waste of time in today's world of science and technology is commonly cited. Can the stark, clinical environment be a true place of healing? Is there a place in the modern world for fairy tales, legends, and other stories?

Storytelling is almost the oldest art in the world, the first conscious form of literary communication. In many cultures, it still survives, and it is not an uncommon thing to see a crowd held by the simple telling of a story.

There are signs of a growing interest in this ancient art, and we may yet live to see the renaissance of the storyteller and the troubadour. One of the surest signs of a belief in the educational and healing powers of stories and storytelling is its introduction into the therapy methods available to doctors, educators, and clergy. It is just at the time when the imagination is most keen, the mind being unhampered by the collection of facts, that stories appeal most vividly and are retained for all time.

Long before pen was set to paper, fairy tales, legends, and stories existed as a means to transfer knowledge from one generation to another. Spreading knowledge through stories was both entertaining and educational. Religious leaders throughout time have used many metaphors and parables to teach valuable lessons of morals and ethics. Some 20th-century doctors believed that such stories contained symbolic messages which spoke to the unconscious of the listener. Storytelling creates a bridge between teller and listener across which authentic communication can take place. And it is within this intimacy that the 'healing' or 'therapeutic' aspects of a story lie. Since the beginning of time, stories have helped us discover the meaning in our experiences, offered possible explanations for what we struggle to understand. Stories invite our imaginations and hearts to stretch over the void to reach out to one another.

Stories and storytelling are appropriate for use at any stage of the healing process. Certain processes are common throughout all therapies; notably diagnosis, establishing empathic rapport, and carrying out a treatment plan. The use of stories and storytelling appear to be particularly effective because they are non-threatening, engaging to both the conscious and unconscious, foster independence, bypass natural resistance to change, model flexibility, make the presented ideas more memorable, and mobilize the problem-solving and healing resources of the unconscious (Dr. Milton Erickson, 1976). Stories and storytelling speak to the normal and healthy core of the individual and can be an instrument of long-lasting and permanent changes.

Storytelling is a sharing experience. When a storyteller shares a story, they show a willingness to be vulnerable, to share ideas and feelings. That kind of sensitivity invites people to listen with open minds and hearts. Enjoying a story together creates a common experience. Storytelling, properly done creates a relaxed, restful feeling. It establishes an environment for the listener to feel comfortable and begin the healing process.

The most powerful and effective way of presenting stories is to tell from the heart and to engage the listener. In this way, the stories and storytelling become an integral part of the healing process.

Storytelling - Skills of the Ancients for Business Success Today

Storytelling has been ingrained in our society and our humanity since the dawn of time. Parents and grandparents have always told stories that embodied their culture. The wisdom of the ancients is captured and passed on in the story. Most great religious texts contain some form of a story. In business, the value of this powerful communication medium is only now being realized.

• Forward-thinking leaders realize the best way to articulate their vision and values is in stories.

• Clever communicators are aware that embedding a key point in a story is the most likely way it will be heard and retained.

• Smart salespeople know that the best way to deal with a client objection is to tell a story about a similar client.

Not a Fairytale... a Fable

Much of the resistance to storytelling in business came from the perception that it's childish - "Storytelling - that's what do with my kids!" It's because we learned some of our earliest lessons through the story - before we could even read - that the story format is so powerful.

Now in business, we're not telling fairy-tales - fanciful stories designed to entertain and amuse. What we are telling are more like fables - short stories with a message at the end.

The format remains the same. While you might not start with the words, "Once upon a time in a land far far away... " if you start your business story by mentioning the time and place it will have more credibility. You probably won't end with, "... and they all lived happily ever after!" But, if you're telling a story to a client to have them change their mind, then you'll only do this with a happy ending!

The 'Great' Story

History is made by the great stories: brave humans who overcame adversity to inspire the world. The stories of Nelson Mandela, Lim Bo Seng, and Malala Yousafzai should be known by every school child. But, in business, these stories, while inspirational, will often fail to get the changed attitude or behavior that we seek. This is because these individuals are so exceptional that most of us can't relate to them. So, the most effective stories are often not the 'inspirational hero' stories, but the everyday stories that they can relate to

Put them in the Story

The most effective story is where the listener can easily imagine themselves as one of the characters. It is a situation similar to one they have experienced previously. This makes it easy for them to put themselves in the story. They create the scene in their mind faster; they are engaged more because it seems so 'real'; but, most importantly of all, they are more likely to see the message of the story as being relevant to them.

The Business Story - Same but Different

Some people say, "I haven't got time to tell stories. My clients say they are busy and they just want the information. They will get annoyed at me if I start telling them stories." This is understandable. Three points to remember:

1. Give them what they need to know - not just what they are asking for. Sometimes there are issues, implications, consequences that they need to understand and the most effective (and efficient) way to do this is through a story.

2. Be time sensitive. A business story needs to be shorter. So, you use only the bare minimum in

set-up and narrative so they will understand the message. This is why success in business stories can often be dependent on your choice of story. If it takes too long to explain in the set-up, then it won't work because you will have lost them before they see the relevance.

3. Don't 'signpost' your story. Whatever you do, don't start with, "Let me tell you a story." They will switch off. Just start the straight in, "I had a client in a similar situation just last month." You'll have them hooked straight away - and they want to find out what happens.

Storytelling is ancient, but that doesn't mean it's out of date. In today's noisy, information-overloaded business world, being heard and remembered is harder than ever. Using the ancient art of storytelling to create cut-through for your message will give your business the edge!

What is Corporate Storytelling?

Corporate storytelling is becoming a new essential leadership skill. It can be used in training and development or succession planning. Through narrative stories, storytelling shares a story about a business challenge, success or experience, while imparting the values and skills of the storyteller.

Storytelling creates an opportunity for active listening, reflection, and dialogue. Stephen Denning, author of The Leader's Guide to Storytelling, states the following seven objectives for storytellers:

- Communicate a complex idea and spark action

- Communicate who you are

- Transmit values

- Foster collaboration and cross functionality

- Tame the grapevine or neutralize negativity

- Share knowledge, information, and wisdom

- Lead people into the future

Storytelling is very different from a lecture focused session. Stories should be presented in a plain, simple conversational and direct style. PowerPoint slides or overheads only distract from the story. After finishing a story, the storyteller or facilitator should invite listeners into the discussion to create a learning environment that shares individual insights and reactions. Listeners should be asked what was learned from the story based on its outcome. Was there success or failure in the story? What can be taken away from the story for a better understanding of how to respond to a similar or different situation within the organization at a later time.

Storytelling is the personal delivery of a case study. The context already exists and does not require building scenarios or simulating the work environment - it is the storyteller's experience retold. To create a personal story, first choose your story by asking yourself these questions:

1.   What story do I want to tell?

2.   What do I want to convey?

3.   What organizational outcomes do I hope to create as a result of my story?

Next, develop your story by creating an outline that can answer these questions:

1. What is the theme of my story?

2. What is the sequence of events in my story?

3. What lessons were learned to help improve the organization?

Storytelling can deliver powerful learning. Is your organization ready to try telling some of its stories?

Storytelling - How Important Is It To Your Brand?

In this 21st Century, there are stories everywhere, more so than before. On television. In newspapers and magazines. Online. Offline. Everywhere we look and see; there is a story. Enhanced by various tools of technological; stories, whether true or 'fake' news, now move more rapidly. They are traversing communities and countries within seconds. Within this quickly changing information environment, for businesses, companies or corporations need to find a way which enables them and their products to stand-out amidst the noise. Therefore, having the "right" story to promote their brand, helps. As an ancient art form, storytelling narrates traditional, cultural and social norms providing communities and countries to express through various mediums. Using the vital elements of plot, characterization and narrative point of view storytelling is used in many ways, as demonstrated through various genres: whether written, theatre, film or video, poetry or music, magazine or newspaper. Compelling, emotional, motivational, inspiring, negative or positive, a story can move the reader or watcher from and through various psychological states.

As storytelling is not new and in business more and in today's business environment some organizations are mastering the ability to tell tales on digital platforms, resulting in positive outcomes on their bottom-line. Creating a connection with businesses and customers, regardless of demographics, the love of a story enables people to make a connection with the narrative.

Therefore, with this connection or 'brand storytelling' will help to transform any content marketing strategy, enabling the content's power to easily engage their audience. It is advisable to invest in telling a story and according to Monte Lutz of Edelman Digital, "as companies begin to adjust to the real-time nature of content marketing, it's easy to lose track of your core brand narrative."

Social media has pushed content to be more authentic and transparent and personal, and storytelling is a part of this swing since at a stories core is a great story that engages the business client or customer's emotions recreating an experience for the audience.

There are many corporate storytelling examples which prove how storytelling can be powerful when done good and well. Emotions sell. Oz Content states: Studies show positive emotions toward a brand have a far greater influence on consumer loyalty than trust and other judgments based on attributes. Advertising research reveals emotional responses to an ad have a far greater influence on decisions than the ad's content - by a factor of 3-to-1 for television and 2-to-1 for print ads. According to Oz, there are eleven great and powerful storytelling examples: Weight Watchers, Guinness, Apple, Google, John Deere, Nike, Lego, Airbnb, Harry's, Warby Parker and Dove.

So how does one create the best brand ever?

- Create the right story by ensuring there is value in the 'human element' content

- Making stories sincere and real;

- The importance of having a Point of View (POV) from the target groups perspective;

- Have an awareness of what connects with potential and present customers

- Defining and identifying positive protagonists, victors, and heroes within the storytelling;

- Keep the storytelling simple, by being able to tell a story in one line.

Finding the human element in a story helps to connect customers to a brand, company or product, so creating a story around that shows how their lives can be better, connecting them at an emotional level.

In today's world, emotional-connecting storytelling content is king resulting in brand awareness and enabling an enhanced bottom-line.

The Art of Storytelling to Create Powerful Brands

"To connect to people at the deepest level, you need stories." Rob McKee

Stories are like viruses.

They are ubiquitous - we all 'get' stories, no matter where we're from. They are contagious - tell a story to someone, and if it resonates it'll spread; the most powerful stories demand to be retold, again and again. And they stick - through the re-telling, they embed themselves in our own and our shared memory.

Anthropologists believe that we've been telling stories for as long as we could speak - they're hard-wired into our brains. They bring communities together, and are our primary way to share understanding and transfer knowledge; that's why they work with children - they intuitively seem to realize their importance, which is why children are so transfixed by them.

We are surrounded by stories - in the media, on TV, the books on our shelves, the memories we share. We tell our friends what happened yesterday or last week, or when we were on holiday, and we're telling a story. Anyone who has put a child to bed at night will know how much they beg for a bedtime story, even one they have heard a hundred times; they are drawn to them, mesmerized by them, feeling that there is something intuitively important about them.

There's an obvious link here with branding. Marketing is essentially about telling stories about the products that we make. Consumers have always subconsciously told stories about the brands they interact with - you just have to sit in a focus group, and it's all around you: listen to the way they recount what a product does, how they describe when they last used it, what a brand means to them or what it has told them about itself.

It's a buzz word now to talk about 'brand storytelling', but look below the hype, and you'll see that it's often simply lip-service, sprayed on; scratch too hard and it'll come off. Since the invention of the brand positioning model, we have created brands in rational and rigid semantic structures, focusing on adjectives and adverbs, most of which are the product of hours of argument over Roget's Thesaurus. Stories take you on an emotional journey, and if we want a consumer to connect emotionally to a brand, a story will resonate more deeply than a set of out-of-context words.

Let's look more closely at what the experts on stories and storytelling have to say about how you create great stories and see what we can learn about making great brand stories.

A critical element of a story is the 'plot'. Things happen in stories. As you watch, read or listen, the story unfolds through a series of actions and events, which drive the story forward to its conclusion. My old Improve teacher used to make us walk forwards when we were improvising a story for us to physically feel the story progressing. 'Story is a metaphor for life, and life is lived in time,' says Rob McKee. Joseph Campbell studied myths around the world and distilled to their most basic elements. A story consists of Order, Chaos, Resolution: everything is fine in the world of the protagonist; something happens to throw things out of kilter; then, after trials and tribulations, things get (relatively) back to normal again.

A story's sense of progression can be seen implicitly in brands - they help us attain something better than we had before. The message or promise at the heart of the brand needs to echo this. Johnnie Walker is a classic example of this: personal progress, drive & ambition are key to this brand; the striding man symbolizes this. Compare Johnnie Walker, about progress, to Chivas, which reflects the status that you have already attained: static. Imagine a film or a novel, where the hero has already achieved what he needed to do - where can the story go from there? He has nothing to do, to show, to experience. So, all brands need to have a sense of progression innate to them - they have to help move us from one state to another, but they also have to evolve in themselves.

The plot captures the activity within the story in a succession of actions and reactions. There have been several books and articles published that explore 'plot,' the premise of many of them being that there are only a limited number of plot types. The most recent has been by Christopher Booker, who believes that every story that has ever been told falls into one of 7 buckets: overcoming the monster; rags to riches; the quest; voyage and return; comedy; tragedy; rebirth. If stories are there to teach you, then each plot represents a different human value and analogously teaches us the consequences of different choices and decisions.

If there are only seven different storylines and every story we've ever told is but a version of one of them, then it would follow that there are only really seven brand story types (which surely would seem to make differentiation difficult, but look at the plethora of Hollywood films that adopt each plot type but dress it up in a different, and sometimes unique, way...) In the same way that Booker professes that storytellers can make their stories stronger by embracing their 'type' (and in some way conforming to the structure and process that it sets out), a brand owner can make their brand story stronger by closely mirroring the construct of their story structure.

Here are a couple of examples of brands that have great stories behind them and which embrace their plot type.

Nike has a strong story of challenging yourself, of striving for your best performance and being committed to the passion for that achievement. For Nike, the only thing to get in your way of achieving this is yourself - the limits of your condition, of your stamina and ultimately of your confidence in yourself. What Nike tries to teach us is that there will be times when it will be difficult, it will hurt, you'll want to give up, but you have to fight through it to win the ultimate battle. Nike's story is of 'overcoming the monster' (just like Jaws, like most Bond films, like Michael Clayton, who overcomes the corporate system...). The monster to overcome is the monster inside you.

The Voyage and Return story teaches us that sometimes life takes us to places that might seem amazing and perfect, but ultimately are ruled by false Gods. Dorothy in the Wizard of Oz is mesmerized by the colorful yellow brick road, but realizes that her life is really at home; Andy, the naïve girl in The Devil Wears Prada, ends up rejecting the false world of fashion that had so completely lured her and taken over how she saw the world. This is Dove's brand story. From its Real Beauty platform, Dove tells us to be wary and distrustful of the beauty industry, and that true beauty is owned and defined by you-you don't have to pretend to be someone you're not. The same way that Andy had to look inside herself and judge whether she was true to herself, so Dove persuades its consumers to be true to themselves.

Other examples: Rags to Riches can be seen in Beetle, Quest in Johnnie Walker, Comedy in WKD or Budweiser, Rebirth in Smirnoff.

To find your brand story, look back at the history of your brand and find the values that are at its core. Look at how and what your brand communicates now. What is the lesson that it is trying to teach its consumers? What is the meaning that lies deep within? Identify which plot type it falls within to make it stronger.

Looking at the 'plot' of your brand can also help to define where your brand is ultimately going, and what obstacles and challenges it might need to overcome.

There is another element that is critical to making good stories: Emotion. "A good story taps into the intellect and emotions of the audience; it leaves listeners enriched in their learning and feelings" (Kaye & Jacobson, 1999). This is what is at the heart of a story - it takes its viewers or readers on a journey, playing with our emotions as we follow the protagonist through his journey. We feel happy when he feels happy; our emotions are plunged when he thinks he's failed; we feel the fear he feels. And a story has to end on an emotional high, something to pay us back for the time that we have invested in it. Likewise, brand stories need to be emotional to connect with your consumers on a deeper, more visceral level. Powerful brands are founded on clear and emotive ideas, and find the emotions behind the brand story, evoking them through all their communications. Think how Cadbury, instead of talking about the joy and pleasure of the product, enacts and shows us joy with the gorilla playing Phil Collins. Think about how O2 is communicating emotionally through its 'We're better connected' platform. ING is moving from telling you about interest rates to showing how fun and playful saving is. Not all emotions are positive... Of the six 'primary emotions' (the ones that anthropologists believe are innate to humans rather than culturally defined) most are negative (sadness, fear, disgust, anger, surprise - positive ones are Joy and Surprise, though this can cross either side). Adverts tend only to show happy people, so what happens when brands center on the other emotions... Marmite showing disgust is probably the best example.

How a brand can succeed and gain a competitive advantage is by telling, and embodying, powerful stories that connect emotionally. If you cannot tell a compelling story about how a product you are designing will be used and the value it will bring to the people who use is, you should question why it is being built in the first place. But, your brand story is not just an anecdote - a few statements and a witty sign-off at the end; stories are metaphors for meaning - they have a 'point' to make. So, your brand story is the sum of all the meaning, character and emotion of your brand.

If you can write a compelling brand story, if you can describe where your brand is going, what it stands for and why it will be what it will be you will build a brand people will connect with, remember & share.

The Importance of Storytelling in Content Marketing

Despite all the distractions of modern life there's nothing we enjoy better than a good story, a skill practically all of us learn at a young age, whether from our parents, grandparents, teachers, and peers, delivered to us sat around a camp-fire, in a lecture hall, over a pint of the good stuff with friends or by way of an immersive IMAX 3D experience, good stories always stick.

With the rise and rise of social media interaction corporations are increasingly required to create compelling 'shareable' content to feed the demand from an increasing number of channels that consumers are using to find and interact with the labels, products, and services they demand. To this end, the art of storytelling is fast becoming a fundamental part of how you can successfully engage with your customers and cultivate your following.

In the pursuit of the perfect narrative, scientific research is delving into the history and the finer details of how good stories can and do change our attitudes, beliefs, and behaviors, and why our brain loves a good yarn.

The importance of storytelling lies in its power to explain, and our brains have long been wired to look for the story when making sense of the world around us. In ancient civilizations those that could explain and most notably embellish the actions of the Gods in times of flood, famine, and war would draw the largest and most attentive audiences, helping to elevate their positions in society and assume positions of authority, thus the rise of priests, judges, rulers and ultimately Alan Sugar, sorry business leaders.

For those in business, today stories can be told using video, arguably the single most engaging format for audiences and one that's fast becoming the preferred way to absorb information. But there's more to just telling a good story than high definition video - if you want a narrative that'll elevate your brand, motivate, inspire and help spread your message the key is in our biology, in particular, the hormone oxytocin.

Oxytocin is a powerful neurotransmitter most commonly associated with relationship building and parent-child bonding. It is produced when we are trusted and shown kindness from others; it helps to motivate us to cooperate with others by enhancing a sense of empathy. Research carried out in the U.S. that involved accurately measuring oxytocin release aimed to understand more about the neurobiology of storytelling and why stories can motivate voluntary cooperation.

Results showed that for stories to motivate people to cooperate in helping others they must maintain attention by building tension during the narrative; if they are successful in doing this they'll not only be more likely to stimulate empathy with the characters but for their audience to mimic the feelings and behaviors of those characters when the story ends. This explains why people are more willing to donate money having watched a charity video.

With an increasing number of businesses making use of video, the neurobiology of storytelling is particularly relevant when understanding what will successfully drive and engage your audience. Wrapping your companies USP's in character driven narrative that can display how you can, or have improved the lives of the characters will help to stimulate empathy from your viewers resulting in a much better understanding of those key messages. Furthermore, they will remember them for longer.

Many brands and organizations have already seen the benefits of how compelling a well-constructed narrative can be upon a target audience, from encouraging people to give generously on Red Nose Day to tell the tale of a startup business. If you want to motivate, persuade and be remembered start with a story of human struggle and eventual triumph. This is what will capture people's hearts - by first attracting their brains.

Despite the many distractions that vie for our attention there's nothing we enjoy better than a good story. Here we look at the hold that stories have over our brains and why marketers are increasingly using the power of storytelling to engage us.

Why is Storytelling Important in Marketing?

Marketing is more than communicating brand messages to audiences, It is a way of engaging with audiences in a way that best appeals to them and allows them to get involved in your brand's journey.

The concept of a brand personality isn't new. Every good brand DNA includes a sense of personality the brand would have if it were a person and if a brand has human-like characteristics, chances are that person has a story to tell. The trick is to find a way to be able to tell that story instead of merely communicating a promotion or sale when you have one.

A brand's marketing or communications team needs to comprise of good storytellers that know how to create greater consumer involvement through emotional engagement. Communicating a sale is ashort-term tactic, while powerful storytelling is the way to create a long-term relationship between the brand and consumer. Humans are connected to each other by their storylines and the point is to find a way for your brand story, and the consumer's one, to meet and move forward together. We are drawn far more to the emotional than the pragmatic, irrespective of what we'd like others to think. Understanding this key human insight will help you build more powerful narratives that connect with audiences more effectively.

Here are few storytelling tips to get you started on your adventure:

1. Be Honest

While it is essential to be able to craft and tell a story right, you need to be telling an honest one. Be consistent and persistent in that truth and build narratives that stay close to your brand promise and DNA - you don't want to confuse your customers by telling a different story each time you communicate with them. Instead, make it as true as you possibly can to a continuing adventure.

2. Be Personal

Storytelling in marketing is very different to conventional advertising. It isn't a sales pitch. You need to first identify and create the persona your brand stands for and put him or her in the centre of the action or plot. You can't tell a boring story, you need to take your consumers on a journey with you and they can only do that if they know who they are following.

3. Be Likeable

If you know your audience, then you ought to know the kind of people they like, and ideally your brand personality needs to incorporate these characteristics. If you want them to root for you, you have to make them like you. Maybe even build in your consumer's personal struggles into the narrative so they can relate to your personality's journey and want to know the rest of the story.

4. Be Linear

If you are telling a story then it ideally needs to have a beginning, a center point and an end as with all good narratives. Open strong to establish your storyline, set up your character's problem in the middle, and ensure that you come to a solution at the end.

The Power of Storytelling

Every day as we are building our businesses, we all know the key to a successful presentation is a product being sold to the end-line consumer and sponsoring a new person. In an upcoming issue, I am going to write about the difference between making a sale and having customer loyalty in the sales process. In the sales process, you are fighting many different types of animals. For most of those who are in direct sales, you have 45 minutes to present a product/business concept and make a person believe in you, your product, and more importantly have them make a decision that they want what you are offering.

When you are presenting the business, it is very easy for you to get very factual and completely lose the interest of your prospect. When you tell a story about the success of someone who is using the product or have a person give a live testimonial about how much they love being a distributor, you will keep the interest of new people who are listening for the first time. For most of us, the first time in our lives that we were ever presented with the concept of a live audience was back in kindergarten when we played "show and tell." Everyone was always interested in what you were saying because you were simply telling a story. We have all heard of the famous K.I.S.S. rule: Keep It Simple Stupid. When presenting your business or product, the key play is to tell a story and keep it simple. Everyone can relate to the grandmother, who can talk about their grandchild as the most beautiful, precious child in the world. She will make you feel as if her grandchild would be such a gift to own as your own. You need to take that same simplicity and utilize it during your presentation and create the same result - ownership of your product. As you tell stories, people will remember those stories versus all the facts in the world.

"FACTS TELL, BUT STORIES SELL." They should want to get involved in your business or purchase your product because of all of the success stories that you told. People love to be part of a winning team. Storytelling keeps people tied into you and your presentation. I always say when in doubt during a presentation, tell a story to bring people's attention back to you. When I present, I ALWAYS tell many stories because when I was first introduced to direct sales, what perked my ears was a story of a young lady who had a lifestyle I wanted. The personal story of her lifestyle is what made me decide to get involved in the business. In that business, I went on to build an enormous organization, and all I did was tell my story and tell the company's story over and over! Combining the key strategy of storytelling along with the correct mindset, you can achieve your wildest dreams!

CHAPTER 2: USING STORY TELLING FOR EFFECTIVE PRESENTATION

The Art of a Presentation

A presentation is a generic term that includes every time someone tells something. It could be a formal presentation to boss and colleagues with the support of technology or can be a story told to friends in a pub. Considering the actual crisis, it could also be a presentation of a job seeker to the Human Resources department of the ideal company. Or a salesperson who has to convince a customer that is the product is the best in the world; even it is not true!

In every situation, the following elements should be mixed and used in different proportions, but every time it is important to use them. One of the best public speakers is Steve Jobs who can use some features to create an effective presentation. In this part of the book, there are highlighted the most popular secrets (most popular and secrets?!?) that are used to present our story, whatever it is.

First of all, it is normal to see persons who are great to tell stories, and then they are not able to

45

say a single word when the boss comes. Or people who could sell a refrigerator in the North Pole, but they are not able to talk to a girl. The good news is that everybody can learn how to do a convincing presentation. To have a prove of that, just check Steve Jobs in his presentation at the university talking about his life and health diseases, where everyone was crying full of emotions and his first presentations decades ago, where everyone was crying but for the horror! After that, everyone can feel better.

Generally, a couple of messages should pass in a presentation: to inform and to entertain. So, it is important to consider what it is said as well as how it is said.

Plan the story

The first step is to be prepared. Planning the plot of the story with analogical support gives the possibility to check the single parts of the story. To do that, software supports are useful, but paper and pens, pencils with different colors and mind maps are much better. The explanation goes more in the mind that is more stimulated the emotional part. Planning a presentation also gives the possibility to insert into it all the possible elements to get the audience attention active. This is the time when it is possible to consider the use of demonstrations, video clips, slides, and every other external element.

The main message

Presentations are used to be remembered by others. Therefore the main message should be clear and easy to remember. To do that a short message is more influenced. TV spots usually use this approach, and some short sentences from the advertisements are commonly used in normal life. Just think a few minutes, and you will be able to think a lot of them. The characteristic they have in common is they are short. We can compare the length as sms or a Twitter message. Even if your message is not told by thousands of people, it must be associated with what you want to say. "The world's thinnest notebook" fits perfectly to MacBook Air.

The story

Like comedians or writers, a presentation is about a story that needs a hero and an antagonist. In this way, the listener can identify himself/herself with the hero and can fell the possibility to fight against the evil. Again, just think to some movies to have a clear example of that. Steve Jobs used IBM as the antagonist in one of his presentation, and Apple was a new force that could save the world.

Audience benefits

The message must have a benefit for who is listening. It could be the best presentation, but if the public is not interested in it, no one will listen. Therefore, the message should be tailored around the audience, and in particular, around the benefit, they can get out of that. It is not interesting for customers that the iPhone can make Apple incredibly reach, popular with a huge market share (that's more important for Apple management). Customers can be attracted by the benefit for them that the iPhone is twice as fast at half of the price.

Rule of the three

Once again, writers use to divide their stories into three parts. It helps to keep the attention high, and it is a good number to remember. Steve Jobs used this rule in his presentation about his life, and everybody can remember those three stories.

Logical plus emotional

It depends on the audience, of course. In any case, a good mix of both should be used. Everybody is impressed by numbers and rational facts, and the emotional factor is usually the winning one. The presentation should convince others with facts: for example, our product is the fastest. And customers must have a good feeling about that, or us. Sometimes a pair of jeans is nice, but we don't buy it because the clerk is not polite. Even more, Steve Jobs likes to sell dreams, not products. It could be like Martin Luther King. In any case, it works, and it is easier to remember. An example could be: "in our small way, we are going to make the world a better place."

Visual impact

Words are important, and images can communicate lots of them in one moment. Even more, a picture can evoke different feelings in the audience. Is the Apple MacBook Air incredible thin? A picture with the Macbook fitting into an envelope is much more powerful. And easier to remember: it has more impact.

Numbers for the audience

Numbers are important because they access to the logical part of the mind. In any case, they must be adapted to the audience. Two hundred twenty million iPods is a meaningful number for sales, not for the customers. 73% of the market share for iPods gives the customers the feeling they are buying the most used product in the market. No number is right or wrong in absolute: it simply depends on the audience.

The emotionally charged event

In every presentation there should be the most important moment, the one everybody will remember. It must be introduced with a sense of suspense, and then the main message should be launched. Prepare your audience to listen to it, or to see that.

Practice makes it perfect

Training is the secret of everything. The first time could be fine; the next will be better. Steve Jobs is an example of that.

Every time there is the possibility to show a presentation. It could be a story or us or our product, whatever. We should be ready at that moment and keep the attention high. Some rules are useful to frame our presentation in a way that will be better remembered by the audience. That's a challenge, but everyone can improve himself/herself getting great results.

The 5 Ws of Effective Presentation

Making a presentation or speaking in public can be a daunting task if not impossible. Even professional public speakers talk about incertitude, nervousness and anxiety every time they have to address an audience. If people who have adopted presentations as their main occupation feel nervous before every presentation, then for the first timer getting the creeps should not be surprising. Most of the uncertainty emanates from what the reaction of the audience will be.

Find below my 5 Ws for making an effective presentation. Indeed there are different ways for calming oneself down before a presentation. This write up, however, is not meant to teach you about handling your nerves before a presentation; this is meant to help prepare adequately for the presentation. The objective is to help boost your confidence and indirectly calm you down for a killer presentation.

The Why:

The first question to ask every time you are asked to make a presentation is to ask why. Why am I making this presentation? You should take time to explore and to understand why you have been asked to speak. There are different reasons for making a presentation. So stop and ask yourself, why you? It may be because it forms part of your work- Job description or that you are an expert in a subject area and so you need to impart knowledge. Answering the why question provides you with a context to which you tailor your presentation. Do you need to inform? Do you need to persuade? Do you need to sell? Maybe you need to teach! Do you need to entertain? Etc. This question must be very clear in your mind. Once you tackle this question, you should be able to structure your presentation to suit the request. This way you are very clear about the agenda, and then you can adequately research to reflect the expectations in the request.

The Who:

To most people, 'the who' part is the most important W among the lot, and it is the one that bothers them. Indeed, 'the who' determines to a large extent how successful or otherwise a presentation is. One important question to ask when asked to make a presentation is to ask who your audience will be. Who am I speaking to? One can have the right words, the right atmosphere, even the right presentation equipment but the effectiveness of the presentation would only be measured by the reaction of the audience. Your presentation must be pitched at the right level for the right audience. The language must be well structured to the understanding of your audience.

A typical example is where a University professor presents two different papers on the same subject to two different audiences. A presentation to his peers on the same subject will differ significantly from a presentation to his students. The question also determines the approach and the tools used in the presentation. The underlying principle is that a presentation is a two-way affair, from the presenter to the audience and from the audience to the presenter. A well-designed presentation, delivered with expertise and skill, crystal clear style, with wit and humor, with the most comprehensive visual aid delivered in the most serene atmosphere will be as dull as dishwater if presented to the wrong audience. Therefore to adequately prepare for a presentation you have to consider the recipient of the message. Ask yourself; who am I speaking to? Who will be in the audience? What do they know about the subject? How many are they? Then tailor your presentation to suit your audience. Research into their background and as much as possible speak to their understanding, not above their heads, neither should you talk down at them.

The What:

The what question addresses your objective. What do you want to achieve with the presentation? It allows you to customize your presentation to address your objectives and the results. To give a good presentation, you need to define what you want to achieve. You can only measure the success of your presentation when you have an objective to which you aim your presentation. It means, giving yourself a goal to measure yourself by. Your objective should be your central message to which other points go to buttress. Defining your objectives also guides the details of your presentation, and you can personalize it to draw out the results. Your objective in a presentation may be to provoke an emotion, to a sales team that has not met its sales target- you inspire, to appeal to your audience for them to release funds, to promote a discussion, etc. Set out your objectives within the four pillars of communication; to inform, to request for an action, to persuade and to build a relationship. The what part provides the framework within which you set out your presentation, and it gives you a yardstick for measuring its effectiveness.

What do you want your audience to do when you finish your presentation. That is your results. Your results must be specific; it must be clear in your mind and must be set out right at the beginning when you prepare for the presentation.

The Where:

The where part of the preparation is pretty self-explanatory. It has to do with location; the arrangement and structure of the venue. You should have a clear picture of what the venue and the arrangement will be. Will you be expected to address the audience in a classroom format, is it arranged to encourage teamwork among the audience, is it arranged to encourage question and answer sections, etc. You also have to research to be sure about the equipment at the venue. Would you have access to a public address system or not? What about a projector, a flip chart, etc.? The nature of the venue also affects your presentation style. You should, therefore, have prior knowledge of the arrangement before the actual date of the presentation. Make a checklist of your needs and make sure that the location can cater to those needs. Where they can't, strategize effectively to address your needs. Surprises right before the presentation can unnerve you and make you disoriented.

The Words:

The words part has two options. Firstly it has to do with the content of your presentation. You must make a conscious effort to structure your words effectively to reflect your research and to fit the requirements of the presentation. You have to research and come up with the best. Arrange your presentation in a structure that you can easily remember. Use words that are easy to understand and you can easily remember. Make sure that you are comfortable with your presentation and as much as possible limit yourself to what you know and can explain better.

The second part is more of advice. That words are not enough. Make use of visual aids. This also means that your speech must blend with whatever visual aids you have to provide a clearer understanding. Pictures they say paint a thousand words and using visual aids reduces the monotony of your voice. You can lecture but make room for visuals and take time to explain. You can also use sound or even video to add some variety or better still, to engage your audience.

What Nobody Ever Tells You about Presenting

Most likely, you've heard this advice: people buy from people they trust. The interesting thing is: what do they buy?

The decision to purchase works for tangible and intangible items--across the board. It's not just for products and services. People buy other things based on trust. Specifically, they buy into advice, ideas, recommendations, and suggestions from those who they know and believe.

What makes you believable to people who don't know you already? A well-structured story.

Your story is the backbone of your presentation. But here's the part most experts won't reveal how to build a story that is real, solid, and true how to structure your story to engage any audience-even if you're short on time and only have minutes to share your ideas.

The 'how' of storytelling is crucial in business presenting. If you tell a story that is authentic, you are very believable. People in your audience pay attention, get curious and want to hear more. Even if you're just meeting for the first time, people feel that you are trustworthy...and they are interested in doing business with you.

If you tell a story that doesn't make sense, doesn't feel authentic, people will have the opposite response. They might not know exactly why. But something just doesn't fit.

This leads people to feel things like:

"Something is off."

"What he said just didn't ring true."

"I felt like there was a piece missing."

What's the result of this? People feel skeptical. They get picky about little things. They may be consciously or unconsciously suspicious. They question everything. Not only your story... but also your words, your background, your expertise, and your recommendations.

In other words, things take a long time and may not move forward. This is not what you want to achieve in interviewing for a job, initiating a consulting job, or sealing a sale.

A strong story is like the spine of any presentation. You may be presenting your bio, your background or your consulting project.

Perhaps you're presenting the story of your company, research or training program.

Many executive coaching clients have asked me, "what are the key building blocks for a great story?"

Here's the short answer. Whatever the topic, organize so your story makes sense for your audience. Appeal to their sensibilities with these eight building blocks.

1. Grabs Attention from start to finish. An instant connection is a secret to outrageous success.

2. Builds Credibility with tangible evidence. From news coverage to press releases to testimonials, share what other people have said about your business.

3. Deepens Interest by providing clear benefits for the audience.

4. Demonstrates Creativity for solving troubling problems and achieving compelling goals.

5. Ignites Desire with a magnetic pull of emotions. Reach deep to find core emotional connection with your audience because people want to do business with people who truly understand them.

6. Confirms Authentic sense that you, your company and your solutions are 'the real deal.' People want to get involved with people who are committed and genuine.

7. Shows Care for your audience. This is vitally important. People want to feel, hear and see that you care deeply about what matters most to them.

8. Inspires Action and decisions. Whether your purpose is to educate, inform, present or sell--action is the outcome.

Structure your business materials and presentations around these eight elements, and your story will have power. Plus, there's an added personal benefit. You'll feel confident, at ease and ready for last-minute presentations.

Imagine the power. A well-built story will boost your business...and your bottom line.

With a logical and creative structure to your story, every presentation is much more powerful. This adds a rush of fresh energy for interactive presentations. The best part? You and your team will feel a boost in confidence...and see a boost in your bottom line results.

A Presentation Tip - Tell a Story

Want to take your presentation skills to the next level? Are you tired of just flipping through PowerPoint slides and boring your audience with data? Start thinking like Aesop and start telling stories.

Presentations based on PowerPoint slides can be deadly, but presentations based on examples, real-life situations and stories can be inspiring and memorable. Most of us can remember dozens of stories from our childhood. A story like, The Tortoise and the Hare from Aesop is a great example. You can never underestimate the power of a good story. Storytellers captivate, motivate and inspire an audience. And great salespeople the world over know and use this power to engage with customers.

The Basic Story Formula

So how do you plan a presentation based on the story and what are the elements of a great business story? It boils down to a simple formula: someone doing something against odds.

Someone can be a person, a company or even a product. The something is an action. And the odds, well, that could be a villain or obstacle or challenge. These are the basic elements of all good stories. Now, how do you put those elements to work?

A Story Needs a Hero or Heroine

A story needs a character we can relate to. Start with describing the main character or actor. This could be someone like Erik Weihenmayer an adventurer who climbed Mount Everest. The character could be a small company struggling to gain market share against a Fortune 500 giant, or a salesperson with a disability like Bill Porter who would not take no for an answer.

Describe a Challenge

One you have introduced your character; explain how this character struggled to achieve something or conquered obstacles against all odds. For mountain climber Erik Weihenmeyer, his challenge is that he is blind! He not only climbs mountains but scuba dives and parachutes out of planes! For Bill Porter, cerebral palsy left him with impaired speech and a pain-wracked

63

body. But that never stopped him for selling in a grueling door-to-door market. The movie of his life, Door to Door, shows how he overcame insurmountable odds to be one of the top salesmen in America.

The best characters and challenges are inspirational, and like Aesop, the audience can see a lesson in the characters as they struggle to succeed. You need to draw that conclusion for your audience: do not assume they will connect the dots on their own.

Relate to Your Audience

The most important part of your story is to make the challenges of the character relevant to your audience. Does your team face obstacles? What could they learn from the determination and resolve of your character? Is the economy a villain working against a small company? What strategy did that company put in place to overcome the economic downturn and succeed? Show your audience HOW they could do the same. Even better, what is your personal story of rising above the odds...your obstacles...your solution? Audiences love a personal story of triumph.

Practice Makes Perfect

Mastering the art of the story can propel your speaking to new heights, but you need to practice. After all, it IS art. Try storytelling regularly in small meetings or staff events to gain feedback on your skills. Get comments on what works and does not. Listen to good storytellers and take mental notes. Keep a journal and fill it with all the great examples of stories that you hear every day.

Present Your Point More Compellingly - Tell a Story

Far from the bedtime stories of childhood or the pop culture of films, novels, and television shows, a business presentation may not seem like the appropriate place for a story. After all, business presentations are where we talk about hard facts. Business presentations are where we let the data influence logical decision-making. Business presentations are no place for a story. Or are they?

Why Stories?

People love stories. They can't help themselves. From the days of our ancestors sitting around the campfire to the modern day storytellers on screen, when we listen to a story, we want to know about the people in the story. We want to know what happens next. Think about it. We've all sat through an awful because we had to know how the story ended. Stories draw an audience into your presentation. Being drawn in helps the audience connect better with you and with your message.

Stories help make the abstract more concrete. In business, we often have to deal with concepts that are hard to visualize if we haven't experienced with them ourselves. A story can help create that picture of what the idea looks like in real life. The more concrete we can make an idea and tie it to something our audience already knows, the more likely our audience is to understand and to remember our message.

3 Tips for Storytelling in Presentations

Make the stories personal.

When telling stories, talk about things you've experienced or observed. That's one way to make sure your audience hasn't just read the story on the internet, in a book, etc. Plus because you're the speaker, the audience wants to hear your insights. Telling personal stories gives the audience a glimpse into who you are and how you think. Stories help them to learn about and like you.

Have a point. When telling a story, be sure to have a point. The story doesn't have to directly relate to the subject you're speaking on, but it should have what presentation skills expert Max Dixon calls a transferable metaphor -- the story needs to have a lesson that illustrates the bigger message you're trying to deliver. The value of the story will be lost if you can't tie the lesson of the story back to the information you provide. So tell the story and make your point.

Include emotions.

When telling the story, including an emotional element that will connect with your audience. Business or not, we're all human beings, and emotions touch us as individuals. While logic may seem the dominate business theme, emotions tie into business decisions too. Adding an emotional element to your story will help strengthen the connection of your audience to your message. The emotion can range from humor to empathy depending on the subject and the point you're trying to make. Regardless of the emotion, stories that touch your audience, whether with laughter or tears, will help make your message easier to understand and more memorable.

A business presentation will always contain the fact and figures that help decision makers make the right call. But using stories can cement the business presentation and make it personal. Use the value of stories to help you connect, communicate and contribute to your next business audience.

Presentation Using "Signature Stories"

It is hard to believe that there are still presenters who will start their presentation with, "Thank you. I am so pleased to be here," or they tell a joke that bears no relationship to their topic. Much stronger is the presenter who has developed strong and effective "Signature Stories."

What Is a "Signature Story?"

A "Signature Story" belongs to you. It can be a personal story about your own experience or experiences. It can be a story about someone else's experience. It can be an original story that embraces the topic and points of your presentation. Or, it can also be a traditional story or fairy/folk tale that has been updated to fit your presentation. I have used all, and with proper preparation, they have all worked to my benefit.

Why Use "Signature Stories?"

Remembering that our "Signature Stories" need to be riveting and topnotch, we will find that as long as we make them unique and "our own," our listeners will react to us and our stories. Good stories are easily internalized, so we as listeners will be able to think back and remember the points made in the presentation. I also enjoy hearing a good story again and again. I remember and love re-hearing Zig Ziglar's cafeteria story, Jim Rohn's Girl Scout cookie story, and Stephen Covey's use of the traditional "Golden Goose" story.

Developing the Personal "Signature Story"

The advantage of developing and using your own story is that it happened to you. That doesn't mean that it doesn't seem plausible and even bring to mind similar stories that your listeners have experienced -- this is even better because they will relate more to you and your topic. It is OK to embellish a bit, but my warning here is to share your struggles rather than your triumphs. People like to hear about times when you are the "bug" rather than the "windshield."

Don't be afraid to expose some of your weaknesses or fears. I have a story that everyone loves called "Bat in the Bathroom." It gets lots of laughs, and many of my listeners rush up after my presentation to share similar challenges with nature's creatures.

One other caveat about personal "Signature

Stories" is that you are not using them for your therapy. I have heard speakers who think they are touching the hearts of their audience when they are making them uncomfortable. I tell a positive story about my son's bout with cancer, but it took me several years before I could tell it without crying. Once I had control and started to tell it -- it is called, "I Believe in Miracles" -- I have had many relatives of cancer patients thank me for sharing it.

So, get busy and develop your "Signature Story." You will be amazed by the presentation power of using it.

Storytelling: The secret to effective presentation skills

A good presentation is one that inspires your audience keeping them engaged from beginning to end; this, however, is easier said than done. It's natural for our minds to wander; in fact, our minds are wandering more than you might even believe – did you know that on average we have around two thousand daydreams every day? One Harvard study has found that we spend half our waking hours with our heads in the clouds and with each of our little fantasies lasting about 14 seconds, our minds are drifting here, there and everywhere! So, the question is – how can you deliver a presentation that stops minds from wandering? The secret to effective presentation skills lies within storytelling. Storytelling techniques are used by some of the most inspirational public speakers and influential presenters in the world.

Why does storytelling for presentations work?

When you hear a story, your brain is put to work. Your brain responds as if it were a real experience. Think about the last time you watched a horror film, were you scared? Think about the last time you read a sad novel, did you cry? This is the reason that stories hold our attention so well, for our brain, the story is processed as if it were happening to us. We are completely and utterly absorbed.

Harnessing the power of storytelling for presentations

So, for the best presentation, all you need to do is tell a story. Easy? Storytelling is an extremely powerful communication tool and harnessing that power can transform your presentations, but chances are you might need a few tips and techniques to help you get the most out of storytelling.

Here are our top 5 storytelling techniques to help you ace your next presentation:

1. Choose the right story

Make sure the story you choose is relevant to the point you want to make in your presentation.

73

Don't just throw a story into the mix just for the sake of it because we said it works. Your story needs to appeal to your audience, to their needs, and their problems. It needs to be relatable. If you're not sure, ask yourself what am I trying to say?

2. Something needs to happen

For a story to captivate your audience something needs to happen, there needs to be some sort of conflict or action. In traditional stories, it's an evil villain that the character needs to defeat; in your presentation it might simply be a problem or struggle that your character needs to overcome.

3. Create drama & suspense

Every good story needs a beginning middle and end. That's what you were taught in school right? Well, it's not necessarily true. Sometimes, a resolution isn't always needed to make a story complete. Leaving your audience hanging can create suspense & drama. It can be especially useful when you're trying to illustrate a point in a presentation too.

4. Get personal

Don't be afraid to be human and show emotion. By getting personal, you open yourself up to your audience. This can make you feel vulnerable but it will allow your audience to feel empathy and understand where you're coming from and this can be hugely persuasive.

Business Storytelling Tips to Guide Your Next Presentation

Who doesn't enjoy a good story? Storytelling is a natural form of communication that is used in every culture. It is an age-old tradition passed down for generations to help others understand backgrounds, beliefs, and experiences. A good story engages various parts of the brain and draws people in, grabbing their emotions, evoking empathy with the characters, and allowing them to visualize the story elements. Listeners stay tuned wanting to know more about the journey unfolding, keeping their attention engaged and imaginations active.

Many scientists believe that humans are hardwired for storytelling. Neuroscientist Uri Hasson of Princeton University is just one expert who has done research showing the effects of storytelling on the brain. Using functional magnetic resonance imaging (fMRI), Hasson and team scanned the brain activity of several participants while they listened to a story. Once the story began, the brain activity of the listeners synced up on a deep level, and "neural entrainment" spread across all brains in higher-order areas including the frontal cortex and the parietal cortex. This deep alignment did not happen during other tests in the study. For example, when the story recording was played backward, the brains showed some alignment of neural responses only in the auditory cortices.

Similarly, listening to random scrambled words from the story or entire sentences cited out of order also did not reach very deep in the brain. Even more surprising, the storyteller's brain activity was studied while telling the story and also synched with the listeners. Hasson concludes that an effective storyteller causes the neurons of an audience to closely sync with the storyteller's brain, which has significant implications for presenters.

Using storytelling as a tool in the business world is gaining lots of traction. However, despite studies on this topic showing how well-crafted stories can be more memorable and persuasive, the value of this art has not been completely accepted or practiced. So whether delivering training about a complex idea, proposing a solution to prospective customers, or presenting a business plan for a new start-up, you'll want to brush up on your storytelling techniques.

To help deliver impactful stories during your next presentation, take a look at these useful tips. Also included are insights gathered from business storytelling professionals' websites that give more perspective on how to put the tips to work.

Understand your audience.

Knowing your audience's pain points and what they value and what they don't will help you tell the right story. Find out what topics interest your target audience or what other brands or people they trust. Try to determine if there are any shared experiences to highlight. Really understanding who you are talking to is a crucial first step in your storytelling journey. Nancy Duarte is the founder of Duarte, a firm that helps businesses realize the power of persuasive visual stories and presentations. In explaining how to identify your target audience, Nancy says, "Make sure you find common ground with the people to whom you're presenting. Common ground helps create empathy; if an audience can relate to the story you are telling them, they'll empathize with you and may begin to care."

Know Your Message

Be sure to understand what you are trying to convey to the audience and how your story relates to the action you want them to take. How do you want the audience to feel about your message? Of course, at some point in the sales cycle, your presentation needs to cover product features. And at some point at the annual kick-off meeting, stakeholders need to hear facts and figures. However, that information should be delivered in an interesting way to make it memorable. Mike Wittenstein founded Storyminers and views stories as a strategic business tool. In an interview blog he explains, "Instead of sharing stories about the numeric outcomes a leader hopes for, develop clear storylines that let people see and feel what the journey of getting to the goal will be like for them."

Ensure your story has a structure

Ensure your story has a structure. A story should include specific periods and names and relatable characters. And it needs to have a beginning (set-up), a middle (contrast or conflict), and an end (resolution and key takeaways). The contrast in the story creates drama. The current frustrations your audience faces can be contrasted with the bright future that's ahead. Consultant firm The Hoffman Agency has a business storytelling blog that sums it up nicely: "...the concept of contrast is one technique that always resonates with participants. The old way vs. the new way. Before vs. after. With vs. without. All deliver a form of contrast that resonates with the human brain."

Be authentic

Business storytelling should not be fictional. If the audience can relate to a real-life story, you are making a connection and building trust. And people like to do business with companies they trust. "Listeners sense authenticity, and if they don't see it, they will reject the story and the teller. The leader's rejected story will become fodder for the powerful 'water cooler' stories and will work against the leader's efforts," explains Molly Catron, an organizational consultant, storyteller, and keynote speaker who works with various businesses.

Use a conversational tone

Use a conversational tone and common words to help your audience relate to you as a person. You will come across friendly and put the audience at ease. Ian Sanders, a consultant, business storyteller, and author advises that stories should be kept simple. You should speak to the business audience as if you are speaking to your friends or family. You do not need to look through a thesaurus just because you're presenting in a business context.

Remember the audience is the hero

The product should not be the hero and neither should the presenter. Your audience should be able to see themselves as the hero in your story. Can they relate to the experience you're telling? The Buzz Factory's Gail Kent talks about how important it is for businesses to tell stories through great content. But, the business needs to act like the mentor and allow the customer to see himself in the story as the hero.

Make human and emotional connections.

Like visuals, emotions also enhance retention. On top of that, research by neuroscientist Antonio Damasio shows that emotions play a vital part in decision-making. His findings have big implications for presenters who are trying to persuade audiences to take action. Doug Stevenson is the founder and president of Story Theater International, a speaking, training, and consulting company that delivers corporate storytelling advice. In one of his keynote speeches Doug explains, "Speak from your head, deliver your content, deliver the message that you know you have to deliver, but keep your heart wide open so that they feel who you are...they have to feel that while you deliver your content." Be approachable, craft a connection aligned to your brand, and think about what you want the audience to feel.

Best Storytelling Tips for Marketing Presentations

What's the worst horror story you can imagine for a presenter giving a marketing presentation? She is falling in love with his or her story!

Recently, I coached a presenter. He was 'all over' stories. And truthfully, his storytelling ability was great if you wanted to sit around the campfire for hours and hours on end.

But, for a business setting, his commitment to 'storytelling' was a death sentence. During his presentation, I looked around the room. People were staring at the ceiling. Others were examining their watches as if they contained hidden gold. No one wanted to hear one more colorful word — not one more elaborate metaphoric example.

Know what I'm talking about? It's the storyteller syndrome. It is gone overboard.

In every part of presenting, there is a risk. You can take a good thing and drag it into the ground by overdoing it.

This does not have to happen. Use these three tips to make sure you use storytelling to your advantage in marketing presentations.

Tip 1: Stick to the Point

In business presentations, unlike campfire stories, you have to stick to the point. Many audiences are filled with people who are already overloaded and overwhelmed with information.

If you want to keep their attention, you must stick to the point. Watch out for any tendency to drift off topic with your favorite colorful examples.

Hint: if this is a problem for you, work with a colleague. If they notice you are going off track, establish a hand signal to mark the moment. Then, be sure to use this signal to refocus your message and stay on point.

Tip 2: Read Your Audience

Read your audience the same way you read the gauges in your car. Are you running on empty? Does your audience need a bio-break? Are they getting fidgety and restless? Are people edging to the door or fixating on their watches?

Watch for the signs and symptoms of disengagement. If you notice these, switch to a more focused delivery style.

You can win your audiences' attention if you keep their signals at the forefront of your awareness.

Tip 3: Let Your Audience Speak

Storytelling is not a one-sided activity. Ask questions. Get people talking. Use their comments and questions to infuse energy and creative spark into your story.

Nothing is as exciting as spontaneous interaction. When you use this in your storytelling, you will not be at risk of talking to a bored or restless audience.

In addition to participants having a chance to speak, other people in the audience often connect with comments made by peers. These comments provoke interaction, discussion, and collaboration.

Professional presenters often use storytelling to express ideas, emphasize key points, and engage audiences. With persuasive storytelling, you can inspire creativity and collaboration.

Effective storytelling is the mark of a distinguished leader and presenter. If you want to connect with your audiences, get familiar with planning, preparing and performing with stories.

As one of my clients puts it: "you get better results with better planning." This is a smart business and a smart storytelling practice.

Develop your business storytelling skills so you can communicate effectively to your audience. Persuasive visual stories can help you reach more customers and grow your business.

The Benefits of Good Presentation Storytelling

There are a lot of tips and techniques you can take advantage of to make a killer presentation. You can come up with valuable content, share interesting data, and make beautiful infographics. Nothing will engage your audience and drive it to action more than a compelling story. This part of this book will explore the benefits of good presentation storytelling that needs to shine in your deck.

Storytelling Creates an Immersive Experience

There are a few reasons that presentation storytelling makes such a major impact. One big reason is that a good narrative will tap into the emotions of your audience and allow them to relate and empathize with the message you're trying to convey much more than facts and figures alone.

That's because, according to the New York Times, when we're told stories, our brains often don't differentiate fact from fiction; instead, we tend to immerse ourselves in the stories as though we're part of them. This, in turn, makes it easier for us to connect to any given idea and empathize with both the message and the person telling the story.

Storytelling Inspires Audiences to Take Action

Humans tend to be driven by their emotions. According to Jane Praeger, a strategic storytelling professor at Columbia University's Strategic Communications and Communications Practice program, "[We] like to believe we are logical, but we use data and facts to post-rationalize the decisions our emotions have already driven us to make."

Therefore, using a strong narrative to tap into the emotions of your audience is a great technique for compelling action. And it's one you can use in any presentation, no matter how dry the data or content is that you're sharing.

Let's say you're presenting about a new product. Rather than focus solely on its features and capacities, walk your audience through how the product came to be. Discuss any setbacks, trials and tribulations, and the defining moments. This will allow your audience to feel more connected to the product and increase their desire to buy it.

Storytelling Makes Your Presentation More Memorable

You can put hour after hour into your preparations, but if no one remembers what you present, all of that time and effort is for nothing. This is where presentation storytelling can step in to help.

Weaving a narrative into your deck is one of the most effective presentation techniques. Ensure your time doesn't go to waste and that your audience remembers your message. In fact, according to Jennifer Aaker, a professor at the Stanford Graduate School of Business, "stories are remembered up to 22 times more than facts alone."

Think about it this way: let's say you watched two presentations about the benefits of meditation.

The first presentation shared health statistics, an analysis of what happens to the brain before and after meditating, and improvements one can hope to gain after practicing it.

The second presentation includes the same information. But the presenter gave a personal account of how their depression made them question whether they wanted to live at all. Meditation changed that completely.

89

Which one are you more inclined to remember? Of course, it's the one with the compelling story behind it.

Now that you know the benefits of good storytelling, are you ready to elevate your presentation game to the next, next level? Then check out this presentation training we've designed to help you do just that.

CHAPTER 3: STORYTELLING FOR BUSINESS PURPOSES

Stories and Storytelling are Good for Business

What do you think of when you hear the term "storytelling"? If you're like most people, your mind may wander through several common scenarios. You may think of a father telling his child a goodnight story. You might remember evenings around the campfires of a camp swapping ghost stories. You might think about those who bring history to life with tales of their long-past younger years. There are so many different possibilities. If you're like most people, though, you'll probably overlook one of the most powerful uses for storytelling. Storytelling for business is growing in popularity and is widely recognized as a powerful communication supplement.

The idea is relatively simple. We all know that narrative structures engage people in very personal and meaningful ways. There's nothing quite like a story to get an idea across. It's been those ways for centuries, and it continues to be true. From Aesop's fables to Zimbabwean tribal leaders, storytelling has had an impact. It's been used so long and so often for one very simple reason: it works like a charm.

Stories connect with us. They interest us. They get our attention. They appeal to our creative instincts, our analytical tendencies, and our creative minds. They do things that "just the facts" approaches can't even come close to rivaling. Storytelling for business merely recognizes that potential and finds an application for it in the professional realm.

That doesn't mean preceding other, more traditional ways of communicating to focus on telling tall tales. Effective storytelling for business requires a bit more subtlety than that. Successful use of narratives in business involves utilizing them to underline key points and to communicate important ideas with an extra level of persuasiveness. Effective storytelling for business can take many different forms, but it's rarely as simple as telling an anecdote to those assembled for a board meeting.

How do we convince the business world that a good story holds more power and is more memorable than hearing and/or reading a descriptive paragraph that relates to an accomplishment, a procedure, a product, etc.? This became so evident recently when I was part of a committee judging nominations for the Regional Company and/or Organization with the Best IT (Information Technology) Training Program.

There were several criteria that we were to grade. The nominees had been asked to write a 250-word paragraph for each of the seven criteria. Most of the criteria were straightforward and asked for descriptions. I could hardly wait, however, until we reached the final one: "Do you have any great Success stories?"

You can imagine my disappointment to find that only one of the nine nominees told us a story. The others blabbed on about profits and accomplishments, etc. The one with a true and moving story -- about a young man who was helped by the training to get a job and a scholarship that turned his life around -- won our vote. The sad part is that I know that every one of the companies or organizations has plenty of success stories. They just don't know how to tell them. What is the solution?

First, don't call it "storytelling." Even though publications all over the nation -- and even the world -- are writing about the companies, organizations, and trainers who are making use of the power of storytelling, very few of the upper echelon will react well to our telling them that they need "storytelling." So many people have the wrong perception of what storytelling entails. They think it is a quaint event that is performed for children in schools or the local libraries.

We can tell them that the World Bank now uses storytelling for information sharing and that a company called EduTech produces a publication called ASK for NASA that consists of employee stories. Todd Post, the editor, writes, "The success we've had with it (ASK) has allowed us to examine our problems holding onto knowledge. Right there in front of our noses was a successful model to emulate." They then created What You Know, which is EduTech's storytelling magazine.

We have to use all of our imagination to work storytelling into meetings, marketing, and everyday encounters. We all know that the stories are there. I suggest taking a small notebook to work or to a company you know well (you may do some freelance work for them or know others who do) and start writing down the casual stories you hear at the water fountain, on the way to an appointment, at lunchtime and in the elevator. Start asking those who had worked a long time at the company/organization about history -- how it was when they were hired and why they have stayed there. When awards are presented, interview those who receive them -- get the full story.

What great success stories does your business have? Start making use of their power, and you will be amazed by how quickly the word travels.

If you aren't using storytelling to your advantage, it's time to broaden your communicative horizons. By learning the art of bringing the narrative to the workplace, you can improve the key points of communication and persuasion. With a little guidance and instruction, you can make one of humanity's most powerful means of forging persuasive connections a regular part of your business life.

The Incredible Art of Storytelling in Branding

Stories came into existence as a human life came into existence. When language was not even invented, or linguistic skills are not acquired, humans conveyed stories through different forms such as carvings, symbols, or paintings. The caves and temples are proof that humans told stories since their existence. Human lives have been reflected in those stories, and people resonate themselves through those stories. Then languages were developed, and other forms of storytelling were invented. From dance forms to writing novels, stories have been told through every possible medium. Humans are more responsive to stories than facts. Businesses need to keep this in mind and devise branding strategies to associate with customers.

The inclusion of storytelling to reach customers has a lot of benefits. The stories about how the business was started, what it stands for, and what change it has made or how it impacted people's lives should be told. There is no end to stories and experiences about any product or service or development process of those products. People relate to stories and stories told based on the theme or purpose of business will resonate with people and it will help in gaining a loyal customer base. This is why Apple has become one of the most valuable brands in the world and has millions of loyal customers. When a new product is launched, people want to use it. Though there are better or advanced products available at lower prices in the market, people want Apple gadgets only. This is because of the story Apple tells about thinking different, staying hungry & staying foolish, and many more. From its foundation in the garage of Steve Jobs to become a multi-billion dollar company, it tells stories, and it does not only sell products but gain loyal customers.

Another important aspect of storytelling is being honest. People can detect lie, and any fabricated story will make a negative impression of a brand. Every business is unique and has a unique story behind it. The individuality must be determined and conveyed through stories. Every person sees the world in their way, but the honest stories touch everyone's heart and help in connective with a brand. The honest expression of a story touches people and elicits a positive response. Moreover, honest stories stand apart from the crowd. This individuality is good for business and branding.

The flow and structure of a story need to be maintained to make people understand the message easily. The complicated structure and lack of flow will confuse people, and it will make a negative impression. There must be a lot of ideation before telling a story and what should be included in the story. If there are elements that connect with people, the storytelling will be successful and favorable for business.

Being one of the leading branding companies in Pune and gaining wide experience in helping brands create awareness, Kaizen Design Studio helps businesses in telling stories in a creative manner that will help them in connecting with customers and creating a good market presence along with standing out from the competition.

Storytelling Techniques in Business - Better Online Communication for Your Business

Once Upon a Time, there was a forward-thinking business that instead of bombarding their customers with facts, figures and sales content, they focused their time and attention on creating easily understood stories that customers could follow, understand and relate to.

As a concept, the method of storytelling within business makes perfect sense. We all know the basics of a story; the beginning, a middle and an end and importantly there isn't a single human on this earth that hasn't heard one. From our first ever steps on this planet we are brought up on stories.

A Story will help us to understand a topic, relate to someone we've not met and help visualize a scene. The medium of storytelling is a great way to engage and maintain concentration levels while also reaching a more emotional, hard-wired part of the human brain.

With websites being the business mode of choice in the 21st Century it is important for businesses to make a good first impression. Another key area is to keep visitors on your site for as long as possible to maximize the chances of a sale, a quote or a contact. Instant statistics from any website are easily acquired; this includes user counts, users decisions/ actions, conversions, etc. Services such as Google Analytics will give highly accurate data regarding any visitors.

The correct implementation of relevant and well thought out stories on your website is much more effective than the old style of information overload seen on many sales orientated websites. With the help of website analytics, the difference can be measured accurately.

Within the digital world, there are some great examples of the story in action. British Telecom's on-going tv advert storyline has created a decent following. BT allowed their followers to get in contact via social media and decide on the fate of the couple featured in the adverts. They had understood the huge benefit of storytelling marketing. Viewers can relate to the situations portrayed and also engage and affect the outcome.

The main aim of online marketing whether it takes the form of the story or the more outdated 'information dump' is to successfully communicate a message that will bring about some sort of behavior change or action as a result.

The storyline approach is best equipped to deliver the following:

- Elucidate your message

- Explain why is Action Important

- Clearly define what Action is required

- What the Benefits and rewards will be

When to Use Storytelling for Business

Storytelling for business is an interesting way to get an idea across. This strategy can be used in advertising campaigns, as well as to put a more human face on the company. Just like humans, a company has a history that suppliers and potential customers are interested in finding out more about.

When an advertising campaign includes a story, it immediately engages the reader or the person viewing it. They follow along and want to know what happens next. They can't help but think that the business using this technique is very creative and has something valuable to offer. Even when the product placement in the ad is at the very end of the story, the viewer or reader is likely to remember what it is and will want to learn more about it. That curiosity is what makes the story a good hook for bringing in new customers as well as making existing ones excited about what your company is doing.

Another way that you can incorporate a story into your business is on your company web site and other materials. Many visitors to the site will want to click on the "About Us" or "Our History" section of the web site to learn more about how the company was established. They will also be curious to find out more about how the business grew from its humble beginnings to the success it enjoys today.

Rather than put out a corporate face that is cold and unfeeling, sharing information about the company and the people who work there makes it more approachable. If customers have the impression that their business is valuable to the company and that their questions and concerns will be listened to and addressed appropriately, they are more likely to come back for their future needs. Tell them about the company's philosophy, the good it's doing in the community or other information that will help the customer feel comfortable.

There are many ways that storytelling for business can help to improve your company's corporate reputation. Using this technique will make it more appealing to customers. You will also notice the difference in your business's bottom line.

Storytelling for Business - Getting Your Point Across

In business, one of the most important factors in success is making a personal connection with those you are working with. Whether you are connecting with customers, associates, or co-workers, storytelling for business can be an important tool in getting goals accomplished. Many think of storytelling as something that is best left for the children's bedtime, but in reality, a good story can have a serious impact on the business world.

Many companies use stories to communicate their vision and roots to customers and clients. By telling a tale of a top-level executive within the company who struggled with adversity and rose to the top of the corporate ladder, they can project hope, drive, and determination. Those who are on that same level can connect with the adversity in the tale and want to contribute to their continued success.

Stories can also be a great motivator in the business world. This is why many companies hire motivational speakers to come into their conferences and meetings to inspire their employees. These people are master storytellers who have rehearsed their tales of finding the ambition to get the job done and done right. Other executives have learned the art themselves, becoming the source of inspiration for their team of workers.

Storytelling can also help within daily relations with customers and coworkers. Because storytellers can draw people in and connect with them through their tales, these people make great supervisors or salespeople. These personal connections are what causes people to gravitate to them and listen to what they have to say. They can persuade a customer to buy or an employee to become more engaged in their work, with just a well-placed story.

Once you see how storytelling in business can have a direct impact on success, productivity, and profitability, you will likely begin to look for ways to incorporate it into your daily business practices. Spoken words can be extremely powerful, giving life to new ideas and allowing you to make a one on one connection with others. Once you have learned to be a good storyteller, you have the keys to success in the palm of your hand.

Effective Marketing through Story Telling

Many years ago, when I was just a young rookie salesman, I was fortunate to fall under the sway of a wonderful veteran sales manager. His name was Milton Lupow, and he became a mentor, teacher, and coach as I struggled to climb the ladder to success. The lessons he taught stick closely to me until this day and at every opportunity I introduce Mr. Lupow's concepts to my clients. When I became a sales manager, then an executive and business owner I appreciated his imparted wisdom even more.

One of the most important, and profitable lessons taught me by Milton Lupow was to sell by telling stories. Ben Franklin closes, take away closes, sales tapes and courses were the rages of the day in the marketing and sales world of that time. Hard selling was common. Mr. Lupow would have none of the trendy techniques.

His sales presentations were seminars in weaving a product's features and benefits, and thus importance to the buyer and their customers, through placing the product in the center of a story. After many successful presentations, as we reviewed the meeting notes, we would discuss the customer's reactions. I began to notice that buyers enjoyed and looked forward to Mr. Lupow's visits as they were not the normal sales blather that was served up by competitors.

Product comparisons, figures, data points, market share and so many other important elements key to marketing and selling consumer products usually do not sufficiently differentiate your product from the competition. Telling stories does. Very few people enjoy being sold something. Everyone enjoys hearing a good story.

After 40 years in the consumer product sales, marketing and product development business I have enough experience to tell stories based on my history. Those many years ago I did not have this chest of knowledge to dip into. I learned to take some element of the product, research and obtain unique elements of origin, geography, harvest, processing, rarity or availability and weave that bit into my story.

For instance, when I was presenting a fragrance I would highlight the unique, exotic essential oils we utilized, how weather affected their price and access and how the flora or fauna that rendered the oils was discovered. Ambergris is collected from the surface of the ocean after whales vomit. Berber women process rare argan oil from endangered trees in the Sahara desert. Many ingredients are harvested in the Amazon by indigenous tribes. A kind of travelogue with cultural highlights frames the provenance of the product as I regularly called on customers I discovered, much as I had experienced with Milton Lupow, that the stories were successful in conveying a more positive image of my offerings. I also found out that I was more welcome each time I returned.

When I marketed pet products, the story might highlight how I had stumbled onto the product concept while watching dogs interact on the beach, or at a park, or my sister's pool party. I invented a wellness pet product by utilizing an ingredient I had found being used in medical surgeries. I had taken a quart of the compound and when placed in sealed, soft-sided bag pets loved to relax on the cooling unit. I discovered this by accident while relaxing at the beach.

If I want to convey how products can jump categories I might tell the story of the famous over-the-counter topical treatment Preparation H. The product was developed by a Dr. Sperti, a Cincinnati-based chemist. It successfully provided hemorrhoid relief for generations. Some enterprising hemorrhoid sufferers somehow discovered that the properties that made the cream so effective in its targeted treatment also made Preparation H a terrific facial wrinkle cream. It became the base for some of the earliest wrinkle creams. That is a real leap.

Several years ago I worked on a gourmet food project. The product was wonderful. But it needed a better story to differentiate it from the competition. We perused the ingredients in the recipe and researched their supply sources. Targeting two key components of the label statement we developed a unique process story about them. We then bought minimum quantities of the ingredients from the most exotic, artesian sources and added them to the product. We now had a unique, rare, quality-driven story about the products special features and benefits versus the competition.

Process stories are excellent tools to utilize for cosmetic, aromatherapy, bath and body, wellness, food, drink, and other consumable products. A proprietary style of production that can be detailed, utilizing a unique engineering or lab process can be a huge difference maker. Ingredient stories alone are rarely enough to achieve success. A trade secret, highly specific method of handling, blending and producing is much more compelling and intriguing to buyers.

Learn to weave interesting stories and points of discovery into your product marketing and sales presentations. Your trade show meetings and sales appointments will be much more interesting and memorable. You will enjoy the increased sales too!

How Stories Can Rocket Your Profits

One of the many benefits of using storytelling in business is that it can communicate powerful messages about you and your product. In today's ever-changing and competitive market, using just facts to send out your important messages wouldn't cut it anymore.

People are looking for that something more that can move and inspire them, something that they can relate to. This is where the benefits of storytelling in business come in.

Since the beginning of time, stories have been used to share information, ideas, history, and knowledge. What makes them work is that they connect with people's feelings.

Humans are not always rational beings. Most of the time, they make decisions based on their emotions. It's important that you understand how you can use this to your advantage.

Stories Simplify the Complex.

Bombarding your potential customers with too much info is useless. After a while, they just tune out whatever it is you're saying, and your words get ignored.

It is important to understand that they will most likely trust someone they can understand. Instead of all these mere facts, tell a story about how and why these can be relevant to them. Not only will it save you time and effort, but it will also leave a good impression on your prospects.

Stories Produce Mental Images.

Facts and figures will be immaterial if they are not able to make an impact. By slipping in all this information in a story and setting your customers' imagination in motion, you can create a strong mental image.

The role of storytelling in business is that it forms the visual imagery that helps capture ideas and increases their ability to be understood.

Stories Help People Cope With Change.

Change is constant and inevitable. Most people dislike change, whether good or bad. Amend this impression by using a story conveying that change doesn't necessarily mean disaster and loss.

An effective way of using storytelling in business is by addressing the customers' fear, uncertainties, confusion or anger through a story that they can relate to. This will help them understand the situation better and create a more positive outlook on it.

By using storytelling in business, you get more of your messages across to your customers. Make yourself memorable to them by being clear and simple. Having a sense of humor can be a bonus too. Don't rely on the facts too much. Remember, the key is to connect!

Storytelling Techniques for Marketing Online

Everyone's heard the storytelling secrets, "Facts tell; stories sell"...

Unfortunately, when I first marketed online, I felt that I didn't have a personal story worth sharing, so I used the "fake it tills you make it" technique.

And hence, this is the problem with online marketing today. We all start from somewhere, and if we all try to fake when we start - then who can anyone ever trust online?

But be me?

They say that storytelling in business on video is the fastest way to success, but the idea of getting in front of a camera and telling my story was scary!

I clicked "exclude this page" on my "about me" page on my first blog that I ever created online because I was shy about coming out with my real story. Now that's part of my story when I make my videos.

I thought, "Why would anyone want to know more about me?"

After blogging for a few years, I found out the hard way that people are interested in hearing stories about other people - both good and bad. And, even if you don't have a "success story" that you believe people would be interested in, there is always some achievement to be found.

You can talk about how you got your first free lead online or how you screwed up your auto-responder and wasted your first 100 leads before learning - but now others can learn from your mistakes.

When you're telling true to life stories in video form, people who follow you get to feel that they know you. And, you know what they say, "people will buy from people who they know, like and trust"... and that's YOU once you can establish an emotional connection!

"That can't be all there is," you're saying... "What are the REAL storytelling secrets?"

OK, here are some storytelling tips to get you started...

1) Determine who you want to influence.

In other words, determine your target market. Try to imagine what kind of person you might be talking to - you know, the kind of person that's going to Google right now and typing in your keyword phrase. Try to figure out exactly what this person is looking for.

2) Determine why you want to influence this type of person.

If find it's easiest to image a single person going to Google and looking for a solution to their problem. I just speak as though I have that solution. Once you do it some times, your speech becomes more confident, and it's not long before you're presenting yourself as a leader.

This person in your imagination has a problem. Identify with their problem but telling a similar story about yourself or someone you know. Be sure to elicit emotion by telling your personal story.

Example: "I remember when I first tried to figure out my auto-responder, and I was so lost I didn't even know what questions to ask to get help"...

3) Determine what it is that you want them to do.

This is where you "bridge" people while keeping them engaged emotionally. Telling a story of how you or someone you know was in this hopeless state with this particular problem, and you found the solution to this problem by watching the same video that they now have access to, etc.

People only want to know that there's hope for them, too. When you can make that emotional connection provide that hope - you just made a new online "friend."

It is a fact that even logical people buy based on emotion. When people listen to you or read your story, they put themselves in the story and connect emotionally.

Storytelling For Internet Marketers

We live in the "Cyberspace Era" where attention span has dropped dramatically. Even those of us who used to loll in a comfy armchair reading a book are finding we can't concentrate for so long.

Have you noticed how you have become a nervous clicker when you are on your computer? Own up. Do you read long articles online? Or do you do what most Internet surfers do, which is to quickly scan, forefinger poised to click through to the next page or website?

If you are in the Internet marketing business, you know you have to get your message across fast.

There is still a place for good storytelling. Our attention spans may be shortening, but we still enjoy a good tale - especially if it appeals to our emotions, our struggles, and our pains.

So if you are trying to make money online, it is good to keep in mind that stories - even very short ones - can help to engage your potential customer or lead.

So much sales copy is bland or over-hyped and relies on popular keywords in an attempt to rank high. It is hard to get around this. But there are opportunities to inject an element of storytelling that might interest your potential customer.

Very often people want to read of somebody like themselves who has struggled and has finally found success. Sure, the rags-to-riches stories have been over-played, but such storytelling resonates.

I have found good storytelling can captivate an audience. As a journalist, I have transitioned from the old school forms of journalism to the modern online copy. I've had news and features stories published that were 3,000 to 5,000 words in length. I've had the chance to include action, anecdote, and description to grab the reader by the throat and pull them through the story right until the end.

Today, as an Internet marketer and a journalist, it is unlikely that I will write a story or article that is longer than 700 words. And much of my marketing focus on short, sharp adverts that have to grab the potential customer and get them to click through to read the sales copy or watch a video with the hope they sign up or make a purchase.

But even in this process, storytelling can help - even in the short text ads that arc so common nowadays.

If you are selling your product, or even if you are selling somebody else's product as an affiliate, you may be able to inject some personality or story into your ad and sales copy. Maybe it is a brief mention of your own story or that of the makers of the product you are selling.

Potential customers need something to relate to. You have to appeal to their emotions. You have to offer them the dream.

You've probably seen this before -

- School drop-out becomes a millionaire

- How I went from debt to riches

- Losing 30 pounds led to success with the girls

- I used to wait tables; now I am a millionaire

- I used to be shy; now I speak publicly to thousands.

Maybe you have a chance in your landing page and in the sales copy for a short story to be told - your story or that of the creator of the product you are selling. Done well, it can help appeal to the emotions of your potential buyer. But it can be tricky because you may be trying to stuff your advert with relevant keywords. You will have to consider what is the right balance between keywords and story.

If there is a story to be told, try to use it.

3 Unbreakable Rules for Storytelling in Email Marketing

How are you telling your business story? Most often email marketing is a core part of how you are presenting your brand and business to customers and prospects.

This week, I got a remarkable email. Sounds funny, right? The reason it was remarkable was this: it was a story that got me to take action.

I don't know about you, but I get a lot of emails. Sometimes over 200 a day. So, when I saw a good story - it made me stop and think. How did they do it? I've found that there are three unbreakable rules for telling marketing stories in an email.

The nuts and bolts of storytelling are simple enough - but it's necessary to understand the mind-set of your customers and clients. Are they strapped to a desk - bored out of their minds? Are they inundated with tons of emails in a cluttered in-box? Are they distracted by personal obligations and family problems pulling on their attention?

Even without knowing you or your clients, there are a lot of business, family, personal and social demands for attention. And you can bet there are a lot of things on almost everyone's mind.

So, the big question in storytelling for email marketing is this:

Why should anyone pay attention to you?

I know it seems a bit harsh. But you must answer this question...if you want to tell a compelling story and make your email stand out.

Let's look at the 3 Unbreakable Rules right now.

Rule 1: Grab Attention In The Headline

Even if you have a terrific story - you have to get people to open your email. The subject line is the single most important part of your presentation when it comes to email.

This is very similar to headlines, magazine covers, and book covers. Sure, you must have something interesting to say inside. But the headline is what pulls people in.

If you want your busy clients to read your story, work on your subject line! Many experts in writing advise spending 90% of your time on the headline. The same kind of targeted focus on subject lines is a smart practice.

Rule 2: Stick To A Single Story

Nine times out of ten: tell a single story. Don't go wandering off in the woods and swamps of your lifetime full of experience. Stick to your story. Avoid adding fancy frills and twists. Stick to your story.

Tell a single story, and make sure it's one that matters to your reader. Do this, and you're going to get a better response...even in an overloaded brain.

Hint: a single story is simple and short. Keep your emails short, and you're in for a pleasant surprise. People are much more likely to respond!

Rule 3: Focus on A Single Action

Yes, it's tempting. Maybe you've got several actions you want your busy client to take. Do not be swayed. Stick to ONE single action.

If you give people several actions to take, what will happen? A big nothing. Too many choices may be your worst enemy.

Instead, keep things simple. One. What could be simpler than that?

Information is a double-edged sword. On the one hand, it can be used to share valuable insights with people across boundaries, across economic barriers, and across time. On the other hand, it can paralyze people into non-action.

But now you know. You know how to focus your emails and inspire people to take decisive action.

Let's just recap:

1. Create a compelling subject line

2. Tell a simple story

3. Provide a single action to take

Not too rough, eh?

Develop your storytelling skills and win results. Tell persuasive stories in email marketing and face-to-face presenting. Discover how to reach more customers, stand out in a crowd, and grow your business.

Storytelling in Marketing: Engaging Your Customers in the Brand's Journey

Storytelling seems to be the ultimate weapon these years in the world of Marketing. At a time when in-bound Marketing is the keyword of every best practices publication, connection with your customers on a direct and ongoing communication basis has jumped from the nice-to-have assets to the must-haves.

What this conveniently broad word is all about, is a blend of immersion and integration: catch the consumers' interest through narratives; make them discover your philosophy and what you stand for through simple messages, and drive them into your brand's history by making them a part of your moves.

One company that got that right over the past years is a leading beverage company that you all know for its sparkling brown soda, and that is already so familiar to every one of us that you would think it doesn't need to invest in communication anymore. WRONG. It remains familiar by regularly talking to its customers and making them act. The marketing team in that company proved it again lately by launching two highly imaginative campaigns focused on interaction with their customers. One of them featured a food truck traveling around the globe, spontaneously drawing customers to stop by and eat together, creating the whole experience by themselves. More recently, the other campaign had participants try to make it to the 6th platform of a crowded train station in 70 seconds, in a James Bond-like race against time, to win tickets for the premiere of the movie Skyfall. Lately, the company launched yet another campaign, printing hundreds of first names on its canned drinks, inviting customers to "share it with... " a person they like.

So what is it that such a massive brand specifically wants to use storytelling for?

First of all, it connects your people and the people you target your strategy. No more vague positioning such as "make it matter" or "make it happen" that confuses even the company's employees, no more one-way messages separating the brand's offering and the customers' expectations.

It improves the efficiency of your communication efforts because people seem to retain information better when presented in the form of a story. Stories and unexpected/uncommon experience with a brand also help to generate buzz marketing and let the story spread massively through your target on its initiative, without you having to spend a dollar on a referral system!

It gives you control over the story of your company and what you stand for: you don't want the customers to build their picture of who you are and risk to miss what's most important about your business, or not make up their mind at all and forget all about your message right away.

And at the bottom line: it helps to significantly increase the dollar value of your products and your brand. A study conducted on over 100 products sold on eBay showed that even at a micro level, stories could increase product value by more than 25 times its original price. Tiffany & Co gained 10% stock value after launching their "What makes love true" brand story. Burberry's stock price increased by 750% since it actively implemented storytelling in its marketing in 2008, through video content and social media.

Three keys to effective Storytelling

To reap the benefit of successful story-based marketing, you have to make it right. Marketers must think like publishers in the way they bring content to their audience and communicate with it. There are several keys to effective storytelling:

Authenticity: in the message conveying the brand's philosophy and values. It establishes the credibility of the company vis-à-vis consumers. Without credibility, the best stories are mere lies that can only drag people away from you;

Content: words, images, sounds, form, characters that resonate with people, through the use of quality and emotional components, mixed with rational elements;

Value added: the search for a reward like in the campaign using James Bond, or entertainment for the watchers. The question to answer is "what's in there for the customer?"

Implementing a story into the brand's communication or product offering may use various ways: from an original and meaningful packaging, like the perfume Paper Passion by Steidl, whose box is actually a book, to retrospective videos such as the LEGO story and bottled whisky brand Johnnie Walker's "keep walking" advertising, both telling the history of the companies with a visual-friendly graphic style or half-humorous tone.

How to Use Storytelling for Business and Why It Matters

Every great speaker is a great storyteller. Why? Because the audience can retain information BETTER when people can emotionally and viscerally connect to what's being said. If you think back to childhood, stories were - for many of us - an introduction to life 's lessons, to human behavior, morals, ethics and right versus wrong. And we remember still the value of those stories and what they taught us, not to mention the vivid imagery they conjure up.

The use of storytelling in business is growing and for a good reason. As the necessity of communicating the value and benefit of what you do to the world increases, the skill with which you articulate that, requires some imagination and uniqueness to capture the audience's attention... and keep it. By activating the imagination of the audience through stories, you, as the speaker, engage the audience to participate in an experience that is both captivating and informative. It's a perfect way to connect to the content of your message. The emotional thread of a story is a direct line to the brain for memory retention and the processing of information. In a sense, you are providing an effortless way to learn using a technique that has been instilled in us since childhood.

Here are some great ways to weave a story into your speech or interview:

•   Be brief. A story should have a strong beginning, a colorful, clear middle, and a great ending. And if the story is within a speech, make it 6-8 sentences. You dissipate the impact of a story if it rambles on too long or is too repetitive. Choose your words wisely and make them count!

•   Paint a picture of a great central character and take us to a different time and place. Set it up well and describe it with a few, choice descriptors. Add a bit of dialogue in the character's vernacular. It will make the character come to life.

•   Know WHY you are telling this story. What is the point of your story and how, very specifically, does it tie into your talking points. Make sure you have the connector! And weave it in seamlessly.

•   Use some dynamic and inflection in your voice when you tell a story. Incorporate some pacing - don't rush. Be a little theatrical (little being the operative word) and let us relish the tale.

And remember your story is NOT your bio. Put that in a document. Your story, any story you choose to use in your business communication should be told with humanity and wisdom, a bit of flair and with a take-away for your audience.

Storytelling for Business - The Surprising Benefits

When most people think of storytelling, images of toddlers cuddled in bed and ready to drift off to sleep spring to mind. While at its most basic, this is precisely what storytelling is, the principles of storytelling can have surprising applications in the real world. Storytelling for business allows messages to be presented in a way that is easy to understand and appealing for a variety of audiences.

Stories allow complex ideas to be broken down into easy to understand terms. Consider the most prominent religious figures throughout the world. Nearly all of them were storytellers on some level. Their talent for drawing in their audience and captivating them into believing that everything they spoke was true and important was what made them into the religious icons seen today. Businesses can harness this same power and draw in customers, or train their employees more effectively.

The personal connection felt between a storyteller, and their audience is what makes this art form so useful in businesses. Trust is a major factor in relationships, whether they are between employer and employee, business and customer, or between coworkers. Good storytellers will gain the respect and trust of those around them, improving their business relationships and making themselves more useful and profitable.

There are two main areas of business where storytelling is the most effective. Stories are useful in customer relations and also in employee productivity training. These aspects of business provide one on one opportunities to connect with others and present important points to them. By finding ways to incorporate storytelling into these efforts, businesses stand a much higher chance of having their message heard.

Storytelling for business will only be effective if you have taken the time to learn just what it takes to be an effective storyteller. Having a grasp on public speaking will give you a solid advantage to put this powerful tool to use. Watch accomplished storytellers in action, then emulate the techniques you see. Once you have mastered this dying art, you can use it to drive business and to improve the performance of your organization's employees.

CHAPTER 4: HOW TO TELL STORIES TO YOUR OWN SUCCESS

Why You Should Tell Your Story

Why worry about your story? So often we tell the story of our business, but disregard the value of the ingredient of our personal story; it's your experience, your struggles and your subsequent successes that can create a real emotional connection to your potential clients or customers.

It is the connection that helps them to see that you are like them that you can understand where they are, and you are living proof that you have the solution to help them with their problem. Video and visual media can put you in the position to create rapport with your audience; your story can secure it, and move them closer to action (becoming a client, customer or even a sponsor).

Of course, we have more than one story, and other stories can be used throughout your marketing, interviews, and videos to create metaphors, highlight problems, and solutions.

The signature story though is one that can be used in visual media to create your following of enthusiastic fans (aka clients and customers).

Three secrets to telling your story with success?

1. Don't disregard the best part; so often that thing that "no one will want to know" or that " you couldn't tell your customers" might be JUST the thing that helps your target market trust you. Idea: journal your most important moments in the development of your business, or career and share them with a trusted advisor or coach. You might be surprised at what will resonate with others.

2. Focus on the recovery, not the problem; It's great to share your struggles and show where you've come from but keep the focus on your recovery and how it has helped you see clearly how to help others. Positivity is attractive and empowering.

3. Be sure to have a few different versions; Have a short version, 30 seconds to two minutes, for networking and introductory videos. Plus, have a longer version that you can share in a longer format, like on stage or you're 'about us" page of

your website. You may even do slight adjustments to emphasize different elements when you are speaking to a select niche audience.

Spend some time on your signature story. It may feel self-indulgent to some, but the ability to help others and increase your business is directly related to rapport with your market, and your unique story is the best way to connect that you've got!

Tell Your Story - People Want to Hear It!

Whether you are blogging for fun or a serious Internet marketer, you have a unique story. How you "tell your story" will separate you from everyone else.

Can you be real and truthful?

That depends on whether your story is real or truthful. You can't tell about your hugely successful Internet business unless it is. You can't talk about your world travels unless you have traveled around the world. If you do, you will eventually be "called out" by someone, and your secret will be exposed. Not something you will want to experience. Let that happen, and your story will never have any value!

You are telling your life story!

What if you don't have an interesting life story or a successful business career? No problem. You can write about somcone else or what you would like to experience by visiting a particular place. Let me give you an example.

"Frank Marino has been one of the most successful online marketers in recent times. He studied and learned video marketing and went from broke to a strong 5 figure monthly income in just a few months. His video marketing techniques have generated over 8000 leads during the past eight months. And he loves to share his unique process so that others can achieve success just like he did."

Frank's story is real and sounds better than mine, so it is to my advantage as an Internet marketer to highlight his life and accomplishments instead of mine. By telling his story, I add value to mine.

Tell your story about your travels!

What if you want to tell your story or a story about a visit to India. I have been there, but this would work whether I had or not. Check it out...

"Imagine seeing heaven for the first time. That's often the experience of many who visit the Taj Mahal in Agra, India. It's mesmerizing, and you can see the love that was put into the creation and then the construction of such a magnificent monument from a grieving man for the woman he loved. A must see in your everyone's lifetime."

By describing the situation and the reason for the building of the Taj, you create a real picture for your reader... one that is believable and worth taking the time to read.

Tell your story... truthfully!

Are you trying to become a powerful Internet marketing guru? Stop stealing space on Facebook timelines, email boxes or article directories with promises that you can't prove or justify. You will just become frustrated, and your audience will tire of your information. Become engaged with your audience. Learn about their needs. Provide solutions for their problems.

Start winning the battle today. Become one of the 3% who is successful online. As Dale Carnegie one said, "You ultimately get what you want when you help enough other people get what they want."

Spend some time deciding who you are. You were made to be special. You are unique. Invest in Yourself. You are worth it.

How to Pitch a Story

Ever wonder why we refer to convincing an editor a story is worthy by "pitching a story?" I have. I'm a baseball enthusiast, and it makes a lot of sense to me. When the editor is at bat with you, he or she has a few swings to make before making a connection – through the story idea (ball) that could end up being a base hit or a home run. Naturally, everyone wants to hit a home run when they go to bat with an editor. Sometimes publicists and writers do have to walk to first base for the story assignment. Here are some helpful tips on how to pitch a story to an editor – and how to at least hit a single, double, or triple – if not a home run on occasion.

Use an Editor's Time Productively

Time spent on the telephone with an editor is more like a gift from God. If you want to be successful at purveying a story idea, it's best to have the information you want to convey rehearsed, or in note written form before your call. Try not to spend more than 10 or 15 minutes speaking about your story idea. Always ask the editor, "Is this a good time for you?" before beginning your pitch. Another great way to reach an editor is by a well-written e-mail pitch. In either case, focus the presentation or conversation on your story idea(s). If the editor is interested, he or she may ask more questions. If not, the editor should tell you.

Facts, Sources, Images

The editor needs to be interested in the theme of your story. A quick 2-3 sentence synopsis should offer an original focus or angle on a topic related to the publication. For example, if I wanted to pitch to Ms. magazine, I'd want to have a feminist event, profile, or feature idea that would be appropriate. Identify potential research sources for your story, or elaborate upon contacts with experts in the area, to let the editor know you are capable of tackling the subject. This expansion on your topic is key to keeping the editor's interest. Many magazine and newspaper editors will also ask you up front about the availability of photographs to go with the story. Be prepared to answer this question with some viable suggestions for photos and a creative approach. By now you've sold the story idea. So, don't forget to ask about the availability of a staff photographer from the publication to assist with photos.

Where do I Find Stories to Pitch?

Whether you are working for yourself or an organization or company, you have your comfort zones. These are vendors you are doing business with, your immediate environment, and social functions that seem aligned with your work. Go outside of your usual boundaries, an experiment in other social venues, and talk to people as often as possible. I look for story ideas when I'm on assignment with a story. Because I write daily, I know that one story will inevitably lead to another. I also pick up story ideas in the bar, at the university where I work as a teacher, from other clients, from students, local activists, or during outdoor group activities such as hiking and camping. I listen closely to what people say, and I carry around my favorite pocketbook sized bungee notebook to record my thoughts and story ideas. When I have an editor on the telephone or am lucky enough to meet one in person, I act like I did when I played ball: I just start pitching.

Tools of the Trade

Once, I had a bead collection I acquired from a friend who was sick of beading. She said to me, "if you just look at the collection long enough, you'll have ideas." This is what I did, and this is how I made my necklaces.

For writers, I recommend they look at as many hard copies and online publications as possible. Don't forget to obtain a copy of the current Writers Market. It's a useful publication for profiling buying publications. I suggest the budding writer look into publications in sync with their interests. For example, I enjoy backcountry hiking and camping. I would probably want to contact outdoors magazines to pitch them some stories. I also have an interest in local newspapers, travel, educational, and holistic healing magazines. I've pitched to all of these types of publications. When you find a publication you like, write down the editor's name, e-mail, phone number and start to pitch. There's also a great writers' site called www.writingformoney.com. For $8 per month, you can review an interactive on-line listing of publications which are currently buying new work. With these links, you can visit the publications directly, read about them, and e-mail the editor your pitch. The longer you look at these tools of the trade, the more ideas will percolate.

Hit a Home Run

You want to hit a home run with an editor and land a story? Well, try going to bat with two to three story ideas instead of just one. Or the story you've developed can be pitched at different angles, which may make it more suitable for your publication of choice. Make sure to view at least several articles from the publication itself before pitching an editor so that you can have an idea of that editor's taste in material and style. All of these tips should help you land a great story, and even more in the future. As with baseball: practice. With practice, you'll learn how to pitch like an expert.

Using Your Story for a Stronger Audience Connection

How Stories Greatly Enhance Your Business Brand Positioning

Have you incorporated your story into your business marketing?

I recently attended a live event, WOW - Women of Worth, at Harrison Hot Springs where several women took the stage to inspire, educate and motivate the audience.

WOW, Event in Harrison Hot Springs 2016 Each of the guest speakers had their own unique story to tell, which captivated the audience and left us wanting to hear more.

What these women did so masterfully was incorporate their story into their presentation. By doing this, they quickly drew in the audience and built a strong "Know, Like and Trust factor" with them.

This immediately positioned them not only as experts in their field but also garnered the trust needed for the audience to take the next step and make a purchase.

And as a result, their "back of the room" sales exploded after their presentations.

Telling your unique story in your business will have your audience wanting more.

Stories Create Fascination

One of the memorable speakers was Leah Goldstein who spoke on Think Like A Champion: No Limits!

Leah infused her story of being a champion kickboxer, a Tour de France cyclist, a Race Across America Champion and the first female undercover sergeant in Israel and instructor of the elite Commando division.

Today she uses her story into her business where she's a motivational speaker and author and also offers wellness weekend workshops, personal and group training and nutritional planning.

How Leah uses her story to build her business compels people to work with her due to the fascination her story brings as well as the proof that she knows what she's talking about!

Stories Help Others Like You

KELITA is another speaker/entertainer who brought her story into her presentation. KELITA is a 5-time Juno nominee and multi-award-winning recording artist, songwriter, comedian, and inspirational speaker.

She had us in stitches laughing one minute and welling up with tears the next! Throughout her time on stage, she took the audience on a journey of her life.

Her story-telling approach had us all not just "Liking" her but LOVING her and wanting to support her; however, we could.

Stories Enhance Your Expertise

Brenda Eastwood brought a different kind of story to her presentation. Her story was based on her 30-year expertise as a nutritionist and how she changed women's lives when armed with the right knowledge about hormones.

By showcasing her expertise through her fact-based presentation plus sharing various success stories, the audience immediately trusted she knew what she was talking about and ran to her table to purchase her packet of recommended supplements.

Another incredible speaker was Olivia McIvor who talked about the Business of Kindness. Her story-infused presentation was similar to Brenda's where she brought the subject of kindness in the workplace to a scientific level, helping us all understand this is way beyond "WooWoo" stuff.

Her expertise was showcased as she brought her 25 years experience in the HR field to her presentation filled with facts, figures and funny antidotes that taught us how to create a culture of kindness wherever we are.

Stories Create Loyal Followers

WOW Organizer Christine AwramEven the event organizer, Christine Awram brought her own story with her where she tragically lost her Mother just a few days before the event.

Her honesty, authenticity and genuine passion for the betterment of the women who attended ensured her not letting this personal tragedy affect their experience was not only awe-inspiring but truly admirable.

Do you think she will get loyal followers after this? You better believe it! Judging by how many women signed up for the April WOW event in Vernon (including me!) and even next year's event again at Harrison was a clear indication of the impact her story had.

Stories Will Build Your Business

Whether you are a speaker/presenter or not, there are plenty of opportunities for you to infuse your own story into your brand positioning for your business.

There are plenty of opportunities you can infuse your story into your business brand positioning

A story will help your audience connect with you on a level that no ad campaign can ever do. Give it a try the next time you write a blog article or write your about page on your website.

3 Methods on How To Tell Your Story So People Buy

As an entrepreneur, one of the most powerful weapons you have in your marketing arsenal is your own story. What do I mean by this? Well, on your website, your personal story should be crafted and conveyed in such a way that it appeals to your target consumers, allows them to relate to you and your business, and prompts them to take action and purchase your product or service. Remember, products don't sell themselves. It is up to you to convince consumers that your product and your business are worthy of their money, and a compelling story is one of how you can do this. How can you make the story that you're telling effective and engaging? Consider one of these storytelling models:

1. The Person-Driven Story:

This is the most common and what I use on my website's About Me page. In the person-driven story, sometimes also called a personal story, an entrepreneur will detail his or her journey to entrepreneurship. This will typically detail a painful, difficult, or challenging problem that an entrepreneur faced and then explain how the entrepreneur was able to conquer the challenge. There are some ways to maximize the appeal of this story. First and foremost, you want to make sure the challenge resonates with your target consumer. In other words, the symptoms, difficulties, or pain you experienced should closely mirror those that the target consumer is likely to be experiencing. For example, if you are selling a supplement to help combat male baldness, you will want to detail your experience with the problem - the insecurity it caused, the toll it took on your relationships, your lack of confidence, etc. If the target consumer can identify with the difficulties and challenges you faced, he or she is more likely to buy into your solution. This kind of story is all about facilitating an emotional connection between the entrepreneur and the target consumer.

2. The History-Driven Story:

The history-driven story is all about research. It will typically detail the history of a particular product or service. For example, imagine you are opening a massage parlor. You might detail the long history of massage, emphasizing its ancient origins and world-renowned healing properties. You then situate yourself and your business as the culminating moment of ever-evolving historic, ancient tradition. The idea is to make your product or service sound exciting, relevant, and worthwhile using history.

3. The Guru-Driven Story:

A variant of the personal story, this focuses on a problem an entrepreneur faced and the "guru" that helped him or her to overcome the problem. Like in a personal story, you will want to focus on a painful, difficult, or challenging problem that you faced and the debilitating symptoms of this problem. However, in the guru-driven story, the entrepreneur doesn't come up with a solution to the problem. Rather, he or she turns to a guru for help, and the guru leads him or her along the path to a solution. Endowed with the wisdom and the insight of this guru, the entrepreneur is now here to help individuals who are facing the challenge that he or she once faced. This helps to boost credibility with the target audience, facilitating a connection.

Keep in mind that these three models are just suggestions. Whether or not you use one of these storytelling formats, keep in mind that a story that sells will always facilitate a connection with the target consumer. It's powerful connections that ultimately work to sell products.

Never underestimate the power of stories. If you need help crafting your story, apply for a Strategy Session so you can be on your way to selling more products/services.

How to Tell Your Story for Your Internet Marketing Business

As a business entrepreneur, one of the most effective ways to connect with prospective customers and team members is by integrating your personal story into your Internet marketing campaign. First timers, however, may find it difficult or intimidating to translate a personal story into words or video. I've developed six simple steps that will assist you in capturing an honest and truthful personal story.

Why do you need to tell your story as an Internet marketer? Simply put, because your story has the power to change someone else's life. Personal narratives give meanings and solutions to the fabric of our common existence. They connect us to our own lives and the lives of others. If told with simplicity and sincerity, a personal story can offer hope to those who find themselves in a similar situation.

One caveat: An embellished or exaggerated personal story may result in the adverse manipulation of the listener's actions or feelings. It can lead him or her to make inappropriate decisions, which will likely hurt them and will it detract from the messaging of your brand.

Therefore, it is crucial that when you incorporate your personal story into your internet marketing campaign, you stick to the truth. A story told with honesty and integrity is more likely to attract the right (read as "profitable") attention for your online business.

Here are six simple steps to transform your story into an effective Internet marketing campaign.

Write a short outline of the key points you want to elaborate on. Don't script it; rather, just jot down the most significant choices you made or actions you took on your entrepreneurial journey toward building an online business.

Sit with a friend and describe how your online business developed. Don't edit, don't judge yourself - just get the words onto a recorder. Any questions your friend asks can help you clarify why you felt the way you did or why you made certain decisions. Which of these had the most impact in determining your future as an online business owner?

Listen to your recording and note which elements most strongly touch the nerve of the inner processes that resulted in your outer successes.

Summarize your story on paper as a sequence of events. Define the situation (sometimes described as the "pain"), the search for an answer, the discovery of the solution, and finally the powerful difference it made in your life. This is the storyboard for your video.

Prepare to capture your personal story on video. An outdoor location is neutral and usually a soothing and non-distracting backdrop for the viewer. Be sure that you record in a well-lit area away from direct sunlight.

Transfer the video to digital format on your computer, and then edit the finished product. Don't try too hard to seem polished. Be authentic and be yourself-your personal story will resonate better with the viewer.

The best way to connect with your target audience is to relate the ups and downs of how you got into Internet marketing in the first place. Those who find themselves on a similar path will be grateful to you for your insight and expertise. Your brand is more likely to be fixed permanently within their minds as the result of an emotional connection.

Remember, the honest retelling of the sequence of events (situation-search-discovery-results) should occupy no more than 3 minutes of video. Don't be discouraged if it takes several attempts to capture it. Keep in mind that the more honestly your personal story is told, the easier it is to rehearse and the more compelling it will be to the listener. Have confidence in what you say, and it will resonate with potential clients.

How to Tell Your Business Story to Increase Your Sales

The elevator speech has as much mystery around it as a Hitchcock movie. It has been talked about and touted as the ultimate skill, so much so that it scares people to give it a go. Let me wipe out those fears and give you a formula for success.

You have probably been being a few uncomfortable situations where a person starts to explain what their business does, and after trying to pay attention to them for 7 minutes, you still have no idea what it is they do or if you would even need what they do. They probably talked about how they package their services or even their hourly rate; they may have even named dropped a few prominent people they have done work for. However, all of this doesn't give you the information you need to know if they can help you or they are just going to confuse you even more.

Sadly, this is far too common a problem with small business owners. They are trying so hard to grasp at anything that will give them credibility that they lose all credibility in their presentation. They are grasping because they don't have a firm grasp of what it is they do. They don't even understand themselves, and if they don't, they sure can't convey it to someone else in a logical and timely manner with confidence.

Let's look at the "elevator speech" and how to craft one that works. The key is in the questions that you ask yourself to reveal your true service and expertise.

What do you do?

What problem do you solve?

Who do you help?

How are you different?

Why is this important to me?

Let's look at the first question: What do you do? It seems basic enough; however, don't fill a page on what you do. Keep it short and to the point. For example, if you are a Realtor, you should state that you are an agent with XYZ. That is it, don't add any fluff this is not the place for it.

The next question is: What problem do you solve? Remember to keep it simple and "Twitter Size" your answer. So in the previous example, you might say, I help people find the perfect home for their needs.

The next question is usually a stumbling block because you have a fear of not being all-inclusive. The reality is no matter what service you offer it is not for everyone. If you have the best steaks in three states and I am a vegetarian, then you have excluded me. If you try to be all things to all people, you will be a master at helping no one. So in the same example, you might answer this buy saying I work with first time home buyers- or you might say you work with retirees looking to downsize. Whatever it is you need to focus on it and use it.

Let's examine the question: How are you different? What is it about you or your service that is unique? What separates you from the other people in your industry? Maybe it is your speed of service or your personal touch. Whatever it is you need to identify it and own it. You might remember a small package delivery service that touted "when it positively has to be there overnight." If you continue with the example, it might be that you have the largest listing of houses in the XYZ school district.

Finally, you need to answer the question: Why is this important to me? Or you could ask why should I, the customer care? Many times business people ignore that what they think is important doesn't mean anything to the customer. This is how you connect with your customer. Get inside their head and find out what is important to them. What keeps them up at night? If we go back to our example, we might say that any new family needs to pay close attention to the school their children will attend.

So let's put our example together so you can see how it works.

Hello, my name is Jane Smith, and I am an agent with XYZ reality. I help first time home buyers find their ideal house. I have the largest listing in XYZ school district because you know how important it is for young families that their children attend the best schools in the area.

That is it. You don't need a diatribe you just need to convey a short message about yourself in a concise and confident manner. Now that you have it in writing you need to practice it until it rolls off the tongue. You may need to practice it 100 times to get the feeling of confidence and connection, and once you do, you can face the world.

CHAPTER 5: A Guide for Perfect Storytelling

The Power of Storytelling - How to Use It in the Business World

Every company and business has great stories. We need to hear them, tell them and internalize them. The biggest challenges, however, are convincing others of the power of storytelling and the impact it can have in the business world. How can we do this?

Start a small booklet of good company/ organization stories. Name the heroes and heroines. Ask others you trust to write up some stories for it. The stories should not be long, but all should include the beginning status quo, a character and characters, the crisis or challenge the climax and resolution, and how the original status quo was changed. Details are important, but should not be overwhelming.

With all of the easy-to-use desktop programs available today, you can put together a small booklet filled with these stories and give a copy to many of your peers. You will be surprised, once the word is out, how many other people will ask for a copy. It may be even time to start a small magazine or company newsletter that consists of stories.

Before a meeting starts (if you have any way of setting agenda items), ask if everyone would share a quick incident that they have recently encountered, what happened and if it changed their thinking and approach. Or ask what was the funniest happening last week. I know it may take some time to get this off the ground -- and, I don't suggest forcing everyone to take part in the beginning.

You will be amazed that if you can continue this quick story sharing introduction, those who haven't contributed before will start having a story to tell and everyone will look forward to this. I know a company that started adding half an hour to the end of their weekly sales meetings for a story sharing session. This soon became the most popular part of the meeting and, as storytellers know, the most valuable part of the meeting.

Once the storytelling starts to take hold -- and it will if you are persistent and keep it going -- the next step would be to call a group of the most enthusiastic story lovers and tellers together to work on the "Grand Narrative" of your company and organization. This will define what your group is all about. What describes the mission and goals in a clear and understandable way? It is OK to redefine your "Grand Narrative" even if you are a large, small, or even a one-person company.

Now is the time to take your storytelling plan to upper management. Convincing reasons that you can propose for capturing and using stories are to accomplish any of the following:

- Share knowledge for succession planning.
- Promote team development to enhance productivity.
- Exemplify values to build community.
- Capture lessons learned to develop best practices.
- Prompt action to change the company or organization.
- Record the past to preserve corporate heritage.

Armed with these purposes and the stories that have already been shared and recorded, you will be able to convince the group that storytelling should be a daily occurrence.

Ten Ways to Become a Captivating Storyteller

People everywhere have one thing in common no matter their language or culture or location on the planet. We love to tell and be told stories.

Stories inform, entertain, grab peoples' attention and reflect their world to them for reflection and in so doing are valuable tools for teachers, speakers, parents and anyone else who wants to interact with others more effectively. Use them often and skillfully and watch people come alive in your presence.

Here are ten effective tips to make sure your stories are told well and captivate your listeners.

1. Be on the lookout for stories throughout your day. Stories are everywhere so carry a notepad with you and jot the storyline down in point form. Flesh it out later. If you have a smartphone with a record capacity, you can use it to record any story ideas that come to you throughout your day.

2. Know the story you are going to tell. When you know the storyline you can play with it to suit the audience. I find that I never tell the same story twice and that's the way it should be. The

storyline remains the same, but the details can vary.

3. Don't rush the story by speaking too quickly. Relax and enjoy the telling if it. It is your moment to shine. There are two temptations to avoid when telling your story, rushing and dragging it out. Be aware of your audience as you tell the story. Their body language will help you judge your storytelling pace.

4. Don't be afraid to make it your own. You can add or subtract details and add texture and suspense with your voice, gestures and facial expressions. In short, you become an actor in your drama.

5. Tell the story don't read it. Anyone can read a story not everyone can tell a story well. When you tell a story, you make a personal connection with the audience and can have the audience spellbound in no time.

6. Use your voice for dramatic effect. It is the instrument you are going to use to establish mood, interest and emotion. If you tell your story in a monotonic voice, your audience will press their snooze button fast.

7. Never let a story drag on and on. You want your story to be short and crisp and to the point.

8. Don't get bogged down with detail. Keep to the storyline. You want to avoid the "Get on with it" response.

9. Insert stories into general conversation whenever you get the chance. I heard the other day... I read in the paper recently about... I saw a man/woman in the coffee shop and... These are just a few of the many ways to insert your story into the conversation. It's great practice for you.

10. Seldom explain your story to your listeners. Let the story speak for itself. There might be times when you can give a brief outline of the story lesson, but usually, it is best to let the story speak to the listener where they are in their life. Often the message you want them to get isn't the message they receive. Who is to say that the message they do receive isn't the one they were meant to.

When the situation is right, it is a bonus to get your audience involved in the telling of the story. This is especially true for speakers, teachers and presenters. You can have great fun with an interactive story. To get an idea of what I mean see the resource box below.

Become a Master Storyteller in 6 Easy Steps

While reading an exhaustive book on the art of storytelling, I discovered a simple and profound truth buried in the final few chapters. It claims that stories will become new products. That one hit me right between the eyeballs. The implications are huge. The world has made a massive shift in the last few years. Value is no longer placed on what I can make, or even, what I know. My value is now entirely determined by my ability to weave my skills, knowledge, and life experiences into a compelling story. "Oh no," you may be thinking, "what's my story?" Here are some tips to help you develop your own story:

Pick a simple, classic story line from myths and fables. People like stories in which they already know the endings. Do you fancy yourself to be a hero, a princess, a champion of good over evil?

Pare the many details of your life down to the stuff that makes sense in the story. There's no need to spill your guts to the universe. People like stories where the hero/in struggles with something but always comes back to their true nature. For example, you are an honest worker who is faced with a temptation of theft, imagines all the things the stolen money could buy, but finally, decides to do the right thing.

Don't think that you are too boring to develop a great story. Some of the greatest myths have been about simple storylines. Read a few fables at the local book store and pick one that highlights the simple things of life.

Share the right juicy details. Only share secrets that help the development of the story and that you are comfortable sharing with everyone. Remember, word travels fast these days and once it's on the internet, it never dies. Ask yourself if you would feel comfortable having your children read this story before you hit the Publish button.

Write for babies. We're all little kids on the inside, and we want to hear how you have triumphed in big and small ways. Use words that are at an eighth-grade reading level to ensure that your audience can keep up with you.

Branch out into the business world. Practice writing a few personal stories first and then write a couple for business. I can think of one person right now who landed a job interview while waiting for the kids at ballet class. You never know when you may need to present a story about your business life to land that next job.

Someone once said that your tattoo is the only thing you ever truly own. Sad? Profound? True? All three? To put a slightly more academic twist on it. Your knowledge is the only thing you ever truly own. And knowledge is useless without a way to share it with the world. Let's take it a little further: your story is the only thing you ever truly own. So then, you are going to need a story that shares your knowledge with the world, gives them an idea of who you are and why they should care.

9 Guidelines for Storytelling in Any Situation

Having a good sense of storytelling techniques is important for people involved in any form of communication. Unlike other ways to express a story, storytelling takes place at the moment between the storyteller and listener. It is a unique experience. Here are nine storytelling tips to use when you want to make the most of the story you have chosen.

1. Choose stories you like.

No matter if you are telling stories to children, illustrating a point in a business presentation or telling a sacred story in church or temple, use stories that you like. There are thousands upon thousands of stories in the world. Use the ones you like.

2. Practice your story.

Take the time to learn how to tell a story. Do not look at or hear a story just once and try to repeat it. Break the story into parts and remember the action piece by piece. Practice with a recording device and a gentle-yet-truthful friend who can hear your first attempts.

173

3. Take out the parts of the story that slow down the action.

Beginning storytellers will hear or read a story and then try to retell every nuance of the story. Storytelling occurs at the moment so not every detail has to be included each time. Ask yourself, "Do I need to tell this piece of the story this time? Is it critical to the story?"

4. Speak clearly.

If you have chosen a story you like, thought about the parts that fit and then practised telling that story, you will be confident of delivering it to the audience. Smile if the story requires it and then speak with that confidence. Enunciate and project your voice towards the listeners.

5. Keep an appropriate pace.

Again, with confidence in your own story and preparation, you will not be in a hurry to spill out the words of your story. Speak slowly enough to be understood but not so slowly that the minds of the audience go wandering.

6. Use a microphone.

You need to use a microphone to be heard. This shows respect to your audience. For experienced speakers, you will want a microphone if your group is 25 or more people. For those new to public-speaking, use the mic with any group larger than a few gathered around a table.

7. Keep good eye contact.

Look at your audience, linger with one person and move on to the next. It always amazes me how one fleeting moment of eye contact can make an audience member come to me and say, "I felt like you were talking to me personally."

8. Use natural gestures.

"You looked so confident up there. I never know what to do with my hands." When people say this to me, I am thankful that I took the time to prepare which gestures I would use and when I would use them. Make gestures that come naturally to you, but plan and prepare them ahead of time.

9. Avoid the "moral of the story" finishes.

Stories are often powerful pieces of Truth and storytelling is one of the most effective ways to convey them. You dilute the power of the story when you are the first to tell an audience what your story means. If you must do the "moral" of a story, ask your audience first to tell you what they think. It will surprise you.

Storytelling techniques like these nine can help you communicate better when you have a story to tell. If you are just starting, choose one or two of these storytelling tips that you will pay extra attention to in your next presentation.

7 Compelling Reasons to Tell Your Story

"We let ourselves loose on that simple blank piece of paper, and our bodies spill. The terror, the love... embodying our stories page after page. In a sense, the pen was our tongue; it is how we delineate the world." Coco J. Ginger

Your Story Can Help Others. Have you been through a life-altering experience? Have you survived something that others might face? Share what motivated you. Chances are you were inspired by someone else's story. Telling your story of perseverance and determination can encourage others to stay the course and forge ahead.

Your Story Can Teach A Life Lesson. Do you know the secret to do something better? Have you found a way to complete a task faster? Do you know a safer way to get a job done? Have you found an easier method for completing a repetitive job? Telling your story of survival or triumph can help others learn valuable lessons while avoiding costly mistakes.

Your Story Can Educate Others. Have you started a business? Did you master a challenging skill?

Have you overcome the (seemingly) impossible? Books are one of the fastest, easiest ways to teach a large contingency of people.

Your Story Can Inspire Others. Have you battled an illness? Have you raised a family? Perhaps you started a successful business or changed a life? Share that information. After all, just as iron sharpens iron, success inspires success.

Your Story Can Instruct Others. How-to books have been best sellers for years for a reason. Teaching others how to do what you do is a time-honoured tradition. Books and workbooks are great teaching tools and resource material.

Your Story Can Preserve Memories. From family history to church history, memories have been shared throughout the ages in the form of stories. Preserve your memories, experiences and laughter in a book. From family folklore to sermon collections to church history, a book is a permanent way to preserve memories and pictures.

Your Story Can Increase Your Business. Business owners and Professional Speakers can increase their income by up to 43% with a simple 100-page book. A book gets in front of people; you might not otherwise see; it brands you as an expert in your industry, and it opens two doors -

one to your target market and one to other professionals in your industry. Professional Speakers with a back-of-the-room product create a whole new revenue stream.

www.ingramcontent.com/pod-product-compliance
Lightning Source LLC
Chambersburg PA
CBHW071232210326
41597CB00016B/2023